# Street Justice

STREET JUSTICE: RETALIATION IN THE CRIMINAL UNDERWORLD is the first systematic exploration of the phenomenon of modern-day retaliation to be written from the perspective of currently active criminals who have experienced it firsthand – as offenders, victims, or both.

Retaliation lies at the heart of much of the violence that plagues inner-city neighborhoods across the United States. Street criminals, who live in a dangerous world, realistically cannot rely on the criminal justice system to protect them from attacks by fellow lawbreakers. They are on their own when it comes to dealing with crimes perpetrated against them, and they often use retaliation as a mechanism for deterring and responding to victimization.

Against this background, Bruce Jacobs and Richard Wright draw extensively on their candid interviews with active street criminals to shine a penetrating spotlight on the structure, process, and forms of retaliation in the real-world setting of urban America – a way of life that up to now has been poorly understood.

Bruce A. Jacobs is the author of two previous books, *Dealing Crack* and *Robbing Drug Dealers*, and is the author or co-author of approximately twenty journal articles and book chapters. He is also the editor of *Investigating Deviance* and the recipient of competitive grant funding from the Harry Frank Guggenheim Foundation.

Richard Wright is the co-author of four previous books, including *Armed Robbers in Action* and *Burglars on the Job*, which won the 1994–1995 Outstanding Scholarship in Crime and Delinquency Award from the Society for the Study of Social Problems. He is also the co-editor of the *Sage Handbook of Fieldwork* and author or co-author of approximately fifty journal articles and book chapters. He has been the recipient of competitive grant awards from the National Institute of Justice, Harry Frank Guggenheim Foundation, National Consortium on Violence Research, Irish Research Council for the Humanities and Social Sciences, and the Icelandic Research Council.

# Cambridge Studies in Criminology

*Editors*

Alfred Blumstein, *H. John Heinz School of Public Policy and Management, Carnegie Mellon University*

David Farrington, *Institute of Criminology, Cambridge University*

**Other books in the series:**

*continued after the Index*

# STREET JUSTICE
## RETALIATION IN THE
## CRIMINAL UNDERWORLD

**Bruce A. Jacobs**
*University of Texas–Dallas*

**Richard Wright**
*University of Missouri–St. Louis*

**CAMBRIDGE**
UNIVERSITY PRESS

CAMBRIDGE UNIVERSITY PRESS
Cambridge, New York, Melbourne, Madrid, Cape Town, Singapore, São Paulo

Cambridge University Press
40 West 20th Street, New York, NY 10011-4211, USA

www.cambridge.org
Information on this title: www.cambridge.org/9780521852784

First published 2006

Printed in the United States of America

A catalog record for this publication is available from the British Library.

Library of Congress Cataloging in Publication Data

Jacobs, Bruce A. (Bruce Abel), 1968–
Street justice : retaliation in the criminal underworld / Bruce A. Jacobs, Richard Wright.
p. cm.
(Cambridge studies in criminology)
Includes bibliographical references and index.
ISBN 0521852781 (hardcover : alk. paper)
ISBN 0521617987 (pbk. : alk. paper)
1. Gangs – Missouri – Saint Louis. 2. Vendetta – Missouri – Saint Louis.
3. Revenge. I. Jacobs, Bruce A. II. Wright, Richard. III. Series.
HV6452.M8 J33 2006
364.1/06/60977866–pcc22    2005024200

ISBN-13  978-0-521-85278-4 hardback
ISBN-10  0-521-85278-1 hardback

ISBN-13  978-0-521-61798-7 paperback
ISBN-10  0-521-61798-7 paperback

# Contents

# Acknowledgments

Contrary to popular belief, academic scholarship is not a lonely enterprise; at least we have not found it to be so. Throughout the writing of this book, we received help, advice, and support from numerous friends and colleagues. We would like especially to thank Eric Baumer, Robert Faulkner, Janet Lauritsen, Bridgette Mack, Rick Rosenfeld, and Volkan Topalli for their wise and patient counsel. Whatever its shortcomings, our book is much better for their constructive comments and criticisms.

Allison Deutsch compiled the index with the sensitivity and insight that have become her hallmarks as a scholar.

The research on which this book is based was funded by a grant from the Harry Frank Guggenheim Foundation. We are required to state that the points of view or opinions expressed herein are ours and do not necessarily reflect those of the Foundation, though the research that gave rise to our views would not have been possible without its financial backing. It took guts to fund such a controversial piece of work, and we are grateful to the Foundation for its support.

Chapter 3 was adapted from Jacobs, B. (2004), "A typology of street criminal retaliation," *Journal of Research in Crime and Delinquency*, Vol. 41, No. 3, pp. 295–323, copyright © 2004. Reprinted with kind permission of Sage publications. Chapter 4 is a revised version of Mullins, C., Wright, R., and Jacobs, B. (2004), "Gender, streetlife and criminal retaliation," an article originally published in *Criminology*, Vol. 42, No. 4, pp. 911–940, copyright ©

2004. Reprinted with kind permission of *Criminology* (The American Society of Criminology).

Finally, Ronald Cohen edited our manuscript with consummate skill, helping us bring to life the hidden world of street justice. The bonus for us is that he did so with patience, tact, and respect for our work. For that, we owe him a special debt of gratitude.

# Preface

Admit it. When someone wrongs you, you want to get back at them. Despite Biblical injunctions to turn the other cheek, most of us are reluctant to do so. The urge to get even is so ingrained in the popular imagination that it has spawned a whole genre of Hollywood movies in which a peace-loving hero is driven to avenge the harm done to a loved one in an explosion of pent-up rage. Think of old classics like *Death Wish*, *Billy Jack*, or *The Outlaw Josie Wales*. Such films were popular because they tapped into a deep-seated human desire to see the good deliver justice to the bad, vanquishing evil once and for all.

The real world of retaliation, however, is seldom as neat and clean as Hollywood would have us believe. It often is difficult to distinguish the good guy from the bad guy in disputes that take place beyond the reach of formal law. Short of death, few such conflicts are ever really settled for good, with each new strike generating a counter-strike in a deepening cycle of instability and violence. Indeed, formal law emerged in part to ameliorate the chaos engendered by retaliation, by replacing informal dispute resolution with a more institutionalized mechanism of social control.

Street criminals, however, cannot realistically rely on formal law to settle their disputes. Despite being especially vulnerable to being preyed on, it is difficult for them to stake a legitimate claim to victim status. Even if the police were willing to believe that street criminals had been victimized – which seems unlikely – strong cultural proscriptions not to cooperate with authorities militate against offenders making an official crime report. Practically speaking, then, street criminals must themselves assume primary responsibility for righting perceived wrongs committed against them.

Despite its preeminent role in regulating disputes between and among street criminals, retaliation has received scant attention from criminological researchers. Existing studies explore retaliation only tangentially, with little or no consideration of its situational and contextual dynamics. Even when retaliation is examined in its own right, the circumstances in which payback is enacted typically receive less attention than the factors that mediate the availability of law. As a result, the structure, process, and forms of retaliation in the real-world setting of urban American street crime remain poorly understood.

This book explores the face of modern-day retaliation on the streets of St. Louis, Missouri, from the perspective of currently active criminals who have experienced it firsthand, as offenders, victims, or both. Chapter One introduces the subject of criminal retaliation, explains why it is important within and beyond criminology, and outlines the research that will inform subsequent chapters. Chapter Two explores the retaliatory ethic among street criminals and the vocabulary of motive that offenders adopt to justify its role as the preferred mode of extra-legal social control. The specter of counter-retaliation, and how grievants perceive and manage this threat, also will be considered. Chapter Three examines the structure, process, and contingent forms of retaliation, offering a typology to organize the data. Chapter Four considers the ways in which gender shapes the context and dynamics of retaliatory events for both male and female street criminals. Chapter Five investigates the phenomenon of "imperfect" retaliation – acts of reprisal committed against parties not responsible for the instigating affront. The reasons for imperfect retaliation and their implications for crime displacement beyond the law will be explored specifically. Chapter Six addresses conceptual issues in retaliation and pays special attention to the role of criminal reprisal in the spread and containment of urban violence.

Throughout the book, and especially in the last chapter, we endeavor to be sensitive to the policy implications of our data.

# ONE

## Background and Methods

THE SKINNY YOUNG DRUG dealer sitting across from us had been robbed at gunpoint. Someone had lobbed a brick through the passenger-side window of his car, shoved a pistol in his face, and demanded his money, drugs, and keys. He handed everything over without protest. The robber had the ups on him – what else could he do? The dealer could not see the offender's face – he was wearing a mask – but he recognized his voice and the distinctive paint-stained boots on his feet. He knows who did it. Now, he wants to get even.

The pursuit of justice animates social life. "[T]he question of what people are entitled to is fundamentally a question about what it means to be a person" (Miller 2001:545; see also Furby 1986). Is it any wonder that people are hypersensitive to infringements on what they believe should be theirs by right, and feel compelled to get even with anyone who dares to deprive them of what they regard as their just due?

The need to retaliate arises from a basic sense of *injustice*, the feeling that you have been unfairly subjected to a force against which you are situationally powerless to act (Marongiu and Newman 1987:9). As "gifts of negative moral value" (Miller 1993:16), injustices create imbalances that cry out for elimination. Though these injustices vary in nature and severity, all deprive grievants of the respect that they believe is owed them (Miller 2001).

Retaliatory urges belie the powerful human need to "get even" (Marongiu and Newman 1987). This desire for payback has been called a universal drive, an instinct, for want of a better term, on the same conceptual plane as hunger or thirst (see, for example, Fromm 1973). We may not wish to acknowledge this "feral force" within us

1

(Seton 2001), but it is there nonetheless, poised and ready to elicit responses against perceived encroachments both major and minor. Someone wrongs you, and you experience a spontaneous urge to strike back, quickly, reflexively, with no qualms. All of us have felt this urge at one time or another. Many of us have acted on it.

The retributive urge has a vicarious dimension as well. The righteous feeling that third parties experience from witnessing wrongdoers get their just desserts often rivals or exceeds the impulse to see victims compensated. As Miller (2001:535) notes, "[H]owever great the empathy that people have for victims of injustices, their anger toward the perpetrator is generally greater." It is not uncommon, for example, for so-called Good Samaritans to leave crime victims bleeding on the sidewalk as they instead chase down and tackle the person responsible for inflicting those injuries (Huston, Geis, and Wright 1976).

Vicarious or direct, revenge is uniquely transportive. It represents a return to the site of an "earlier moment of pain." The objective, of course, is to neutralize that pain for, in its perpetual remembrance, there "can be very little freedom to accept the future" (Barreca 1995:9). Such neutralization is obviously impossible because harm – once inflicted – can never be undone. Revenge, therefore, takes on a certain "magical" quality (Fromm 1973; Marongiu and Newman 1987).

People have long taken the law into their own hands in an attempt to right perceived wrongs. Historically, vigilantism served as the principal method by which disputes were resolved. It remains the prevailing mode of social control in traditional, honor-based societies, triggering penalties that can be notably violent. "Honor societies," as Gould (2003:126–127) remarks, "are renowned ... for the practice of blood revenge." He continues:

> Social scientists interested in explaining the practice ... have most often seen it as a form of dispute resolution – a tool for settling conflicts in situations lacking a formalized, third-party justice system. It is now commonly argued that the threat of revenge is a functional alternative to the threat of third-party punishment;

according to this view, social groups, usually families of some kind, can deter rival groups by making it clear that the kin of someone killed during a dispute will punish the offender and possibly others in the offender's group.

Be that as it may, the retaliatory ethos that underpins traditional blood feuds is backward-looking in that it encourages individuals to bear grudges, to remember past wrongs, and to disregard their future well-being in favor of getting even (Gould 2003).

As societies modernize, there is a move away from informal methods of dispute resolution toward a more bureaucratized system of justice that allows individuals to transfer their grievances to a formal authority and thereby get on with their lives. As Gould (2003:22, 170) puts it: "Honor systems encourage people (especially men) to react quickly, definitively, emotionally, and often physically to insults or other transgressions, whereas the modern bureaucratic world emphasizes dispassionate, rational deliberation and long-term planning. ... [In modern societies,] prudence and peacemaking demand ... that wronged persons abandon the past and embrace the future." Even in modern societies with highly formalized systems of justice, vestigial contexts inevitably remain. The street criminal underworld is perhaps prototypical in this regard: It exists largely beyond the reach of formal law and continues to lionize honor – often in the guise of "respect" – as something to be protected at all cost.

Offenders who fall victim to crime are reluctant to go to the police because, among other things, doing so could expose their own illegal activities to official scrutiny. But even if criminal victims could make a police report without fear of implicating themselves (say, through a guarantee of immunity from prosecution), few probably would exercise this option; most realize that the government cannot enforce illegal contracts. Moreover, the inherently conflictual relationship between street criminals and law-enforcement personnel, coupled with an informal code that prohibits offenders from cooperating with authorities as a matter of honor, militates against turning to the police for help.

Street criminals' desire for safety and justice are of little or no concern to most police officials anyway. As a result, offenders are forced to handle conflicts and disputes through a rough-and-ready brand of self-help (Black 1983). The need for them to retaliate is substantial because street criminals are especially vulnerable to victimization. Living in high-crime neighborhoods, largely invisible to the police, often carrying high-value contraband (for example, drugs), dealing almost exclusively in cash, and regarded by virtually everyone as deserving what befalls them, street criminals are routinely exploited by other predators. The only realistic mechanism available to them for responding to such attacks and deterring future ones is exacting their own justice.

Cultural imperatives reinforce the need for retaliatory justice. In the volatile world of street crime, projecting an image of self-reliance dominates almost all other concerns. Inter-personal encounters are loaded with meaning, especially disputes, which are proving grounds for character (Oliver 1994; Anderson 1999). Violations that do not elicit retaliatory responses label the victim as being weak, and on the street, there is no place, or mercy, for cowards (Topalli, Wright, and Fornango 2002).

For precisely this reason, alerting the authorities is not a realistic option for criminals who have been victimized. Calling the police stigmatizes you as someone who cannot handle your own business. Cooperation with the authorities also may label you as a snitch, and in street culture there is no more reviled status. "[A] snitch is the worst thing you can be," one street criminal proclaimed, "inside or outside of jail" (quoted in Rosenfeld, Jacobs, and Wright 2003:298). Being labeled as a snitch, deservedly or not, can result in your being targeted for retaliatory strikes, and many an informant has experienced the wrath of jilted street criminals looking for payback against the "rats" who supposedly implicated them.

The paradox of criminal self-help is that it occurs in a setting inundated with law enforcement. Zero-tolerance policing in its many guises – saturation patrol, crackdowns, sweeps, covert operations, and the like – is emblematic of the War on Crime that has taken over the nation's urban neighborhoods. Such tactics are

4

divisive at best, sinister at worst, but all foment a general perception that the police are the enemy – individuals who abuse their power and exercise discretion for purposes best considered nefarious (see, for example, Miller 1996). When the source of a sanction threat is perceived as being unjust, the sanction loses its assumed legitimacy and generally cannot have the desired deterrent effect. Worse yet, attempts to impose an illegitimate sanction may actually encourage individuals to defy it and commit more crime (Sherman 1993). At the least, this will decouple the link between formal and informal social control – the building blocks of collective efficacy and crime containment – and allow instability to thrive. This reinforces the code of the street and the retaliatory ethic that drives it.

Although retaliatory acts committed in the name of social control are a widely recognized feature of the urban street scene, they seldom appear in official police reports despite the fact that many of them clearly represent serious violations of the law. An understanding of retaliation as both a social process and a control process is important, however. It is clear that a substantial number of assaults, robberies, and other forms of serious criminal behavior are a direct consequence of retaliation and counter-retaliation (Topalli, Wright and Fornango 2002). As such, retaliatory conflicts contribute significantly to the violent reputation and reality of many high-crime neighborhoods. Retributive threats play a crucial role in shaping the interactional environment in which street-level behavior is enacted, motivating offenders to acquire firearms for both retribution and protection. This leads to a concomitant increase in the number of firearms on the street, the diffusion of firearms to persons not directly involved in predatory crime, and an increasingly casual use of weaponry (see Blumstein and Rosenfeld 1998; Jacobs et al. 2000). Retaliation fuels official rates of serious violence, resulting in injuries or deaths that cannot easily be covered up (Jacobs, with Wright 2000). This may trigger a contagion of violence, whereby increasing numbers of disputants get sucked into germinating spirals of conflict. The resultant instability and chaos can have grave long-term consequences – within the street criminal underworld and beyond it.

Despite the potentially destabilizing influence of retaliatory justice, knowledge of the perceptual, situational, contextual, and interactional mechanisms that mediate its occurrence remains incomplete. We are not the only analysts who find it startling that so little empirical criminological research has been conducted on the topic (Vidmar 2001:33). The absence of inquiry is all the more striking when readers consider that most social control is informal and that many crimes are moralistic in nature (Black 1983; Katz 1988). Retaliation represents the obvious intersection between informal social control and moralism. It is, in the elegant parlance of Donald Black (1983), "crime as social control."

Exploring the intersection between crime and informal social control facilitates a more precise understanding of both deterrence and the contagion-like processes through which violence is contracted and contained (Loftin 1985). If, as some have suggested, the spread of violence represents a public health problem (Cook and Laub 1998; Mercy, Rosenberg, Powell, Broome, and Roper 1993), then we must identify the precise mechanisms that facilitate or impede its transmission from one event to another. Not only might this lead to a better understanding of how cycles of urban violence are promoted and intensified, it also might suggest key points of intervention to break these cycles before they spin out of control (Jacobs, Topalli, and Wright 2000).

The most promising way to address these issues is to go to street criminals themselves. They have an insider's view of how street crime and informal social control interact in a hidden world beyond the law, outside the popular preoccupation of most academic criminologists and criminal justice policymakers.

## Our Study

This book explores the perceptual and situational factors that mediate retaliatory decisions in the real-world setting of urban street culture, where the ability to exact payback carries especially strong sub-cultural currency. To this end, we recruited from the streets of St. Louis, Missouri, fifty two active offenders who have participated directly in retaliation and interviewed them at length about their behavior, paying particular attention to factors that condition the etiology and enactment of street justice. By attending to what Katz (1988:3) calls the "foreground of criminality" – that is, the perceptual mechanisms through which retaliatory acts come to be contemplated and carried out – we will illuminate links between criminal lifestyles, victimization, and the immediate social and situational contexts in which decisions to strike back are activated. Retaliatory decisions, after all, are not made in a socio-cultural vacuum; they are embedded in an "ongoing process of human existence" (Bottoms and Wiles 1992:19; see also, Jacobs and Wright 1999).

Our exploration of criminal retaliation is anchored conceptually at the nexus between rational-choice theory and phenomenological interactionism (see Wright and Decker 1994). Rational choice is a paradigm that holds that all human decisions emanate from a process of careful calculation and assessment. Actors weigh the costs and benefits of anticipated behavior, and proceed when the latter exceed the former. While this ultimately requires actors to make a subjective evaluation of prevailing conditions, decisions revolve around a set of external objective properties that, to a greater or lesser extent, are predictable. In contrast, phenomenological interactionism attends more to the transient internal emotional states that underpin decision-making in the offending moment (Wright and Decker 1994). Sensual concerns predominate, and cool rationality gives way to hot "emotionally-laden" cognition (see, for example, Exum 2002). This often results in less than optimal choices, though at the time they may appear optimal to the party making them.

Blending rational-choice theory and phenomenological interactionism, then, permits us to assess the simultaneous impact on retaliatory decisions of hard, verifiable contingencies (for example, costs, benefits, physical obstacles) and subjective emotional forces (Jacobs, with Wright 2000). This approach is critical because the structure of reprisal, its process, and contingent forms inevitably reflect elements of both calculation and emotion. Ascertaining the relative contribution of each has important implications for understanding the role that retaliation plays in facilitating – and constraining – the spread of street crime and violence.

## Research Site

The research on which this book is based was conducted in St. Louis, Missouri. Once a manufacturing hub for the Midwest and Mississippi River Valley, the city is now in serious economic trouble. The revitalization that swept through so many other rustbelt cities in the 1980s and 90s largely bypassed St. Louis, a city with a long and complicated history of regional political fragmentation that has habitually inhibited economic development. Lucrative blue-collar jobs, once the principal source of high-paying employment in the city, have vanished, and nothing of real consequence has replaced them. Residents of St. Louis have fled, and continue to flee, to the surrounding suburbs, taking much of the tax base with them. In the forty years following World War II, St. Louis lost more than half its population (Bray 2003). A significant portion of the remaining population is poor, aging, and in chronic need of expensive social services.

Against this backdrop, serious crime and violence flourish. St. Louis consistently places at or near the top of large U.S. cities in rates of violent crimes such as armed robbery, aggravated assault, and homicide. In 1999, for example, the city ranked first in total crimes per capita among American cities larger than 100,000 (Hackney et al. 2000). Recent FBI statistics indicate that 2,323 serious violent crimes per 100,000 people were committed in St. Louis – over four times the national average (UCR 2002). The city's murder rate (nearly seven times the national average), robbery rate (over six times the national average) and aggravated assault rate (over four times the national average) are among the highest in the nation. Property crime rates, including burglary, larceny, and auto theft, are over three times the national average. Increases and decreases in St. Louis's violent crime rate tend to mirror those of other U.S. cities, albeit on a different scale. This makes St. Louis an ideal laboratory for investigating the dynamics and processes relevant to violent criminal events, including retaliation (see Rosenfeld and Decker 1996).

## Sample and Recruitment

As already noted, data for this study were drawn from in-depth qualitative interviews with fifty two active street offenders. A number of these individuals were interviewed more than once, and one of them had to be eliminated from the sample because of the poor quality of the interview, producing a total of sixty six separate interviews. Interviews took place over a 22-month period that began in summer 2001. The mean age of respondents was 27 years (the median was 26). Forty respondents were male, twelve were female; respondents, on average, had completed 11.6 years of formal education; twenty five of the fifty two respondents claimed to be working in some legitimate capacity at the time they were interviewed; thirty six respondents reported having children; five of the fifty two respondents were married. All respondents were African-American.

We chose to employ qualitative data-collection techniques because they are ideally suited to the study of "hidden populations" – groups difficult to access by virtue of their stigmatizing or illegal behaviors, which members actively work to conceal from outsiders (see Spreen 1992). Qualitative methods permit investigators to explore the conduct norms that underpin the behavior of hidden populations. In addition, such methods reveal emergent behavioral and decision-making processes, an especially vital objective when the people or setting being examined reside at the "forefront of broader trends" that require real-time identification for the formulation of effective social policy (see Golub and Johnson 1999:1737).

Studying criminals "in the wild" is not an easy task. Offenders have strong incentives to hide their identity and activities from outsiders. This makes them difficult to find, and, once located, they often are reluctant to cooperate. Such reluctance is reassuring in the sense that it helps to confirm potential interviewees' deviant status as lawbreakers. For street criminals, the price of indiscretion can be high – lost freedom, reputational damage, even death – so their suspicion of strangers is understandable. Perhaps the most common suspicion that street criminals harbor about outsiders is that they are undercover police of some sort. As Sluka (1990:115) notes, "It is difficult to find an [ethnographer] who has done fieldwork who has not encountered this suspicion." This is hardly surprising; in the street criminal underworld it is a "basic cultural rule ... to treat everyone as a snitch or the man [police] until proven otherwise" (Agar 1973:26).

Many criminologists opt to study incarcerated criminals instead of active offenders because doing so can be easier and more convenient. Finding prisoners obviously is not difficult (though negotiating the bureaucratic obstacles necessary to gain access to them may be), and the tedium of prison life ensures that many of them will cooperate, if for no other reason than to break the monotony of their daily routine. The drawback to prison-based research is that jailed offenders represent a certain type of criminal – those who have been caught and successfully prosecuted. By definition, this makes them unsuccessful criminals and perhaps different from offenders who have managed to evade capture. Beyond this, prisoners often bring an agenda to the interview setting that can compromise the validity and reliability of any information they provide to researchers. No matter how much they are assured otherwise, incarcerated offenders often associate researchers with prison staff and other criminal justice functionaries who can provide benefits or mete out punishment. Bias results when prisoners tell researchers what they think they want to hear in the hope of receiving a reward or avoiding a penalty. Many inmates steadfastly believe that "what they say to researchers will get back to the authorities and influence their chances for early release. And even if this does not seem likely, why take the chance? Consequently, inmates ... put the best possible spin" on their previous activities (Wright and Decker 1997:4). For these reasons, criminologists have long "suspected that offenders do not behave naturally" in criminal justice settings (Wright and Decker 1994:5). Sutherland and Cressey (1970:68), for example, point out that "those who have had "intimate contacts with criminals 'in the open' know that criminals are not 'natural' in police stations, courts, and prisons and that they must be studied in their everyday life outside of institutions if they are to be understood." Polsky (1967:123) similarly cautions that "we can[not] afford the convenient fiction that in studying criminals in their natural habitat, we ... discover nothing really important that [cannot] be discovered from criminals behind bars." Human beings, after all, are animals. They are no more likely to behave naturally in captivity than polar bears or aardvarks. Imagine going to a zoo to study the hunting strategies of lions.

As a practical matter, jailed offenders also have a tendency to recollect their crimes as having been far more rational than they really were. Their rationality is reconstructed "in a manner consistent with what 'should have been' rather than 'what was'" (Cromwell et al. 1991:42), an artifact of the controlled setting of the prison interview room, coupled with the distorting lens of time that can imbue even the craziest of behaviors with purpose and meaning. The "prison environment is detached from [the] temptations and pressures" of street life, so research conducted in such a setting inevitably misses the powerful role those forces play in shaping offender behavior (Wright and Decker 1994:213).

Respondents were located through the efforts of a specially trained field worker who has collaborated with us on several previous projects, going back five years. When we first met him, this person was an active criminal and a respected figure in the St. Louis underworld. His direct involvement in crime attenuated over the course of time – he got older and wiser and, by his own admission, tired of running the streets the way he used to – but he retained a solid reputation among his criminal peers for integrity and trustworthiness. Walker and Lidz (1977:115) remind us that access to clandestine worlds requires an "individual who will establish the [researcher's] credentials [and who is] well thought of by the other participants in the system." Without such a person, research of the kind undertaken here has little chance of success.

The field worker recruited individuals whom he knew to be involved in street culture and crime, and asked them to participate in an interview. The types of offenses these individuals were involved in ranged widely, from assault to property crime to drug dealing and use. We chose not to reveal our specific study protocol or interview questionnaire to the field worker prior to initiating recruitment for fear it could give interviewees an opportunity to craft their responses to meet the needs of the study. All of the respondents had experience with retaliation – as victims, perpetrators, or both – some of it quite extensive and recent. That experience was the main focus of our interviews.

Interviewees were paid a modest sum for speaking with us. On the street, time is money and nobody ever does anything for nothing. In past studies (see, for example, Jacobs 2000; Jacobs, Topalli, and Wright 2000; Wright and Decker 1997), we paid $50, an amount deemed sufficient to generate participation without unduly influencing would-be respondents to cooperate. This time, limited resources prevented us from paying all interviewees that amount, but participants were adequately compensated relative to market ($40) when they did not receive the full $50. Respondents who did not receive that amount were told that others before them had indeed received more. We wanted to inhibit the introduction of bias caused by a perception of relative deprivation by claiming, honestly, that our budget simply would not allow for a $50 payment in every case. Though any sum of money over a few dollars may be perceived to be excessive, it is important to keep in mind that most of our respondents could have earned much more had they spent the time "hustling." And, from their perspective, committing an offense probably seemed less risky than revealing their participation in illegal behavior to strangers.

We cannot claim that our sample is representative of offender networks in St. Louis. Those networks vary along a number of dimensions, including, among other things, structure, hierarchy, and density. Offenders in St. Louis tend to be "urban nomads," living nowhere in particular but "staying" or "resting their head" in many different places depending on mood and circumstance. Mobile offenders, in contrast to those who stick close to their own neigh-borhoods, provide greater scope for tapping into these diverse net-work dimensions. Though a sample size of fifty two may seem small, it should be noted that previous studies have relied on fewer informants with notable success (see, for example, Mieczkowski 1986; see also Humphreys 1970 on "the intensive dozen"). The absolute number of respondents is less important than the process by which they are selected. As one anonymous reviewer put it, five, if selected prudently, can be more than adequate. If selected poorly, 100 may not be enough.

We employed three broad eligibility criteria to select our respondents. We sought respondents who (1) had been actively engaged in street crime in the six months prior to being contacted (that is, had committed one or more offenses that typically are considered street crimes such as drug dealing, drug use, assault, burglary, robbery, carjacking); (2) considered themselves to be active street criminals; and (3) had been the victim of at least one crime for which they had retaliated, or attempted to retaliate, in the previous six months. We have used analogous inclusion criteria for prior studies of crack dealers, drug robbers, and residential burglars, and they have proven to be appropriate, effective, and useful (see, for example, Jacobs 1999, 2000; Wright and Decker 1994, 1997).

Verification of eligibility is one of the most important facets of research of the kind undertaken here (see, for example, Biernacki and Waldorf 1981:150). We tried to ensure that our respondents met the inclusion criteria, but there were practical limits to how far we could go in doing so. This is where the project field worker's knowledge of the offenders he recruited – their reputa-tions, activities, patterns, and so on – became especially important. Because of his extensive street knowledge and connections, the field worker was best positioned to gauge whether prospective respon-dents were appropriate for us to interview. Careful questioning of the interviewees helped us to monitor his success, as did occasional "Q-and-A" sessions with the field worker himself (to confirm or disprove something a respondent said). Some of our respondents failed to meet all of the inclusion criteria, but it is important to remember that qualitative researchers must retain a degree of flexibility in their recruitment strategy so as not to exclude potentially valuable informants (see Wright and Decker 1994). Thus, we elected not to send away offenders who had committed their last retaliatory act more than six months ago, or who were not heavily immersed in street offending at the time we interviewed them when, during the interview, we could establish the retaliatory incident's ongoing salience (cognitive, practical, or both) or the particular respondent's substantial history of offending and involvement in street criminal culture. Such flexibility can have the unintended benefit of increasing variance in the sample as well as substantiating internal validity. For example, respondents may be more willing to disclose highly incriminating or threatening details relating to an event that occurred in the distant past as opposed to something that happened recently.

## The Interviews

Interviews were semi-structured and conducted in an informal manner, allowing the offenders to talk freely using their own concepts and terminology. Conversations were consensually tape-recorded and transcribed verbatim. The resulting transcripts were coded manually using standard qualitative techniques of domain analysis and constant comparison (see Glaser and Strauss 1987; Spradley 1980). Questions focused on the offenders' most recent retaliatory experiences, and the events that led up to them. By concentrating on recent events, we attempted to maximize recall while minimizing the distortion that can compromise accounts of behavior that took place in the distant past (see Loftus and Hoffman 1989). That said, a number of respondents described incidents that took place long ago. Due to their violent or remarkable nature, such incidents remained salient, and respondents' descriptions of them were sufficiently detailed to warrant analysis.

To guide our interviews with the offenders, we deconstructed the retaliatory process into a series of closely linked, sequential stages, beginning with the instigating affront and ending with the act of reprisal and any associated counter-reprisal. The basic value of this organizational scheme centers on its ability to pinpoint the key objective and subjective processes that shape retaliatory episodes throughout their evolution.

Because one of our aims was to explore the procedural dynamics of violence (see also Luckenbill 1981; Polk 1994; Hagan and McCarthy 1997; Jacobs 2000; Wright and Decker 1994, 1997), we tried to sort out the sequencing of retaliatory events as well as the foreground dynamics that triggered discrete episodes. In a few cases, this required us to explore how retaliatory incidents were linked across time in order to account for the larger inter-personal and social context in which disputants were embroiled. Social status differences between disputants, relationships between conflicting parties, and the presence or absence of third parties were factors explored to this end (see Black 1983; Gould 2003).

It is inevitable in research of this nature that not all respondents will be asked the same questions in the same way, or in the same order. This is especially true because we conducted the interviews over a two-year period, and those that took place later in the process tended to be shorter and more focused, owing to our desire to pursue particular issues raised earlier in a more systematic fashion. Our interviewing style – which is decidedly conversational – is to blame as well, but this is the best way we know to generate "thick," or highly detailed, descriptions. On many occasions, the most valuable data come from the "small talk" that permeates all such interviews. We did not wish to inhibit the flow of conversation for the sake of adhering to the requirements of a formal interview schedule. Taking this path means that some respondents will speak about issues that others do not; in some cases, the ratio of responders to non-responders will be decidedly skewed. These and other imperfections are unavoidable in research based on semi-structured interviews, but they need not be damning. As Van Maanen (1988: 56–57) notes, "[A]bsent evidence of fallibility, the fieldworker may appear too perfect and thus strain the reader's good faith" (see also Wright and Decker 1994:23). Polsky (1969:132) suggests that, far from being problematic, this is a strategy researchers must actively pursue:

> [T]o impose on the field worker some of the controls that purists want – to insist that different field researchers ... must each ask their subjects exactly the same questions in exactly the same order in exactly the same words ... is severely to contaminate the very thing we want to study, the reactions of people in their natural environment.

An additional word about our interviews – they tend to be fairly chaotic affairs. Almost all of them take place in a large conference room at our urban university. Our field recruiter escorts each respondent to and from the campus. Sometimes respondents insist that the recruiter be allowed to sit in on their interview. We always accommodate such requests, politely asking our field recruiter please not to say anything; not infrequently, however, he breaks his promise to keep quiet, underscoring a point made by one of the respondents by blurting out something to the effect that, "that's the way it is out there, there's some crazy motherfuckers on the streets." Other times he falls asleep almost immediately and snores loudly throughout the entire interview. Occasionally, he brings his one-year-old son with him and everybody – respondent and interviewers alike – ends up playing with the baby.

For all of the difficulties associated with allowing the field recruiter to sit in on interviews, things are worse when he stays outside. Our field recruiter is not a patient man, and within a half hour or so of our starting an interview, he invariably begins knocking on the door, asking us when we will be finished. "I got things to do, man. I got to baby sit. When you gonna be done?" No matter how many times we ask him to leave us in peace, he continues to interrupt us every five or ten minutes until the interview ends.

We sought to develop and maintain strong rapport with each of the individuals we interviewed, but we were not entirely successful. College professors and street criminals see the world differently enough to ensure that things between them do not always proceed smoothly. Even during the most amiable and animated conversations, there were moments when we antagonized or failed to connect with one another, sometimes on purpose, but more often inadvertently. Over time, we came to view rapport not as something we could establish firmly, but rather as a transient state of mutual understanding that fades in and out as people with very different backgrounds struggle to find common ground.

## Validity: External and Internal

It is impossible to determine the extent to which our sample is representative of the total population of active criminals, but it clearly over-represents African-American offenders. This reflects our field recruiter's own racial status. There is a real divide between blacks and whites in the St. Louis criminal underworld. The city's population is about half white and half black, but only about 13 percent of the census block groups in St. Louis reflect this balance. The remaining block groups are either almost entirely black or entirely white (Bray 2003). Because racial groups so strongly self-segregate, it is difficult for our field worker to recruit whites – he simply does not cross paths with them. The heterogeneity of the sample with regard to gender, however, is not problematic; our field worker recruited a strong contingent of women.

Questions about external validity plague virtually all purposively derived data that, by their nature, result from sampling on the dependent variable. The "positivist nightmare that research participants, individually or collectively, may not be 'representative' or worse still, that they may be exceptional or idiosyncratic, runs deep" (Maher 1997:29). Sampson and Raudenbush (1999:607) claim that this is one of the most enduring concerns in the criminological community, referring to it as a "fundamental cleavage of sociological criminology."

The external validity of a sample drawn from street criminals at large in the community can never be determined conclusively because the parameters of the total population are unknown (Glassner and Carpenter 1985). Local characteristics of communities vary, and so do particular offenders' experiences with, and accounts of, retaliation. Yet it is important to recognize that the traditional phone or mail survey method would never be able to collect the kind of data we assembled here. Inefficient and poorly targeted, household surveys are unable to generate respondents in reliable numbers (Heckathorn 1997:114; for a similar discussion of these problems, see Jacobs, with Wright 2000). This is especially true when the target population consists of transient street offenders, who are unlikely to have a reliable mailing address or a working telephone. Then there is the pervasive suspicion of outsiders that is characteristic of all street criminals, and that undoubtedly is stronger when the research instrument is an impersonally administered questionnaire as opposed to a face-to-face interview arranged by an indigenous and trusted field worker. As we mentioned earlier, the more sensitive and stigmatizing the desired information, the more important such "personalized" techniques become.

Although our sample cannot be generalized to the total population of street criminals, it may still provide a window into how such offenders think and act in real-life settings and circumstances. St. Louis is a particularly good place to do research of this nature. Its middle-of-the-country location and moderate size make it different from more popular criminological research sites such as Chicago, Miami, New York, or Los Angeles. St. Louis is arguably a more typical American city than megalopolises such as New York or Los Angeles, and the findings generated here may have a greater degree of policy relevance for a greater number of places (Jacobs 1999).

Internal validity is always a concern in interview-based studies of individuals engaged in serious wrongdoing. In talking to researchers, such individuals may perceive themselves as putting their freedom on the line; how can we know that they are being truthful? The answer is that in the absence of direct observation – which in the case of lawbreaking is neither ethical nor safe – we cannot know, at least not for sure. Nevertheless, the validity and reliability of offender self-report data have been examined by a number of scholars, all of whom have concluded that in-depth interviews are an excellent method of generating valuable information (see, for example, Elliott and Ageton 1980; Erickson and Empey 1963; Nye and Short 1956). Indeed, the best data are said to result from face-to-face interviews, the strategy used here. This is not to say that offenders never exaggerate or lie about their activities, only that they do so less often than is commonly presumed (see Fleisher 1995; for an overview of these issues, see Jacobs, with Wright 2000).

In addition, we view some degree of offender dishonesty in interviews to be almost desirable; it serves as an unobtrusive measure of their deviant status as criminals. In that sense, complete candor would be cause to doubt their authenticity. It is also important to recognize that offenders often lie or exaggerate about things that we are not empirically interested in. In many cases, this means adding "color" or excitement to descriptions of events for the benefit of us, their audience. For example, an offender may exaggerate the description of a police car chase by telling us about being pursued by ten police cars all over the city, whereas only three such cars were actually involved. The number of police cars is less important than the fact that there was a chase.

We took several steps to maximize the data's internal validity. First, we promised all respondents anonymity and confidentiality, and we did not record any information that could identify anyone by name or link him to a specific incident. For example, we instructed respondents not to use the real names of anyone involved in a given event, nor to give specific locations or addresses of places in which they had committed offenses. Street names were recorded, but these monikers tend to be sufficiently generic to apply to a broad range of individuals rather than to any respondent in particular (over the course of our research with street offenders, we have spoken with three "Blacks," three individuals with "Little" in their first names [Little Dee, Little Rag, and Little Tye], and four individuals with "Dog" in their names [Ray-Dog, Big-Dog, Smoke-Dog, and Dog-Ass]). We also told respondents that their comments could end up in a book, so it was critical for us to "get it right."

Previous books we have written about crime in St. Louis are featured prominently in a display case right outside the interview room, validating our claims and also providing an excellent way to "break the ice." At least three respondents interviewed for this study were quoted in one or another of these books. We opened the relevant book and pointed out their transcript-excerpts, which were met with smiles, nodding approval, and a genuine sense that what they were telling us "really counted." We attempted to monitor the truthfulness of responses by identifying answers that appeared to be ambiguous or contradictory and asking the respondents to clarify what they were saying. We underscored our longstanding relationship with the field worker who had recruited them because if he said it was safe to confide in us, he was usually believed. Our reputation on the streets of St. Louis as "all-right squares" (Irwin 1972) is so widely known that offenders have, in the past, voluntarily contacted us (either directly or through our field worker) to talk. One respondent boldly called us two weeks after being interviewed to volunteer his services as a contact person. Recognizing that our studies were "legitimate," he wanted to move in on our recruiter's action. He brought in one respondent free-of-charge to prove himself, and offered to bring in several more at reduced cost. Because the study was nearly complete, and because we feared undermining our longstanding relationship with the field worker, we decided not to take him up on his offer. The general point we are making is that we are recognized and trusted among the circles of offenders from which we recruit and, as a result, rapport is not a problem.

More often than not, respondents relaxed soon after the interview began, engaging us and sometimes even leading the conversation. Many genuinely seemed to enjoy speaking to us. The opportunity to talk with someone "straight" (non-criminal) about their lives may be rare for those immersed in street culture and crime. Offenders often find that the opportunity to talk to someone outside their criminal fraternity is liberating. As Wright and Decker (1994:26) have observed, "The secrecy inherent in criminal work means that offenders have few opportunities to discuss their activities with anyone besides associates, a matter which many find frustrating" (see also Letkemann 1973). Offenders almost always have skills and knowledge that researchers lack, and this puts them in a position to teach investigators – people who reputedly are "smarter" than they are (at least in terms of educational attainment) – a thing or two about street life (Jacobs 1999). Offenders desire social recognition for their competence in much the same way as do law-abiding citizens (West 1980), and paying them for information that only they can provide represents a tangible acknowledgement of that competence (Wright and Decker 1994:26). If offenders see something in the research that benefits them, or look at the interview as a venue to correct false impressions about who they are or what they believe, accurate responses will come more easily.

Interviewing disputants involved in the same retaliatory event would be the ideal way to check the validity of what each respondent told us. But this strategy was not practical – both for ethical and logistical reasons. Recently, Topalli, Wright, and Fornango (2002) interviewed offender/victims of violent crimes and found substantial overlap between their accounts of victimization and retaliation and those of previously interviewed offender/victimizers (Jacobs, Topalli, and Wright 2000) regarding the ways in which such offenses were executed and how cycles of retaliation and counter-retaliation played out over time.

Qualitative researchers are ultimately themselves best positioned to gauge the veracity of offenders' reports because they *are* the research instrument (Wright and Stein 1996). In this regard, it is important to note that we have an intimate knowledge of street culture and crime in St. Louis. We share eighteen years of experience studying active street criminals there and, collectively, have interviewed more than 300 offenders over the last decade-and-a-half. We have extensive experience "on the street," and understand local activity patterns. As a result, we are well positioned to verify that what respondents tell us reflects the day-to-day reality they confront.

When it comes to the issue of internal validity, iron-clad proof will always be elusive. But this is where field work with active criminals comes into its own. In past projects, respondents have shown up for interviews carrying firearms, bleeding from a recent gunshot or stab wound, or carrying probation papers. One woman interviewed for the current project came in with a six-inch long scar across her throat and a second four-inch puncture scar right above her heart (both suffered about a year earlier in a drug deal gone bad). Other individuals eagerly displayed battle scars when asked, mostly small caliber gunshot wounds that had since healed, albeit imperfectly. One person we were supposed to interview got so high on drugs before coming to speak with us that he could not climb the hill that leads to our office (we interviewed his associate instead). Yet another respondent was released from twenty-hour "lock-up" just prior to our interview; arrested for fighting, he had yet to take the shoelaces out of his pocket and re-thread his sneakers (corrections officers customarily seize the laces for safety reasons and give them back when the offender is released). Such incidents testify to the type of respondent we recruit and bolster our confidence in the sampling technique and data collection strategies used here.

## An Editorial Note

This book draws heavily on excerpts of transcript material. Obviously, such excerpts represent only a small fraction of what the respondents actually said. "Selectivity is an unavoidable problem in the textual representation of any aspect of social life – criminal or otherwise – and it would be naive to claim that this cannot distort the resulting manuscript" (Wright and Decker 1997:31). Selectivity also means that we draw more heavily from some transcripts than others. Indeed, a few interviewees are not quoted at all, though they remain part of the sample because they nonetheless inform the analysis. Some respondents inevitably are more candid, articulate, or knowledgeable than their counterparts (Prus 1984:253), and reliance on them is necessary to fully explicate the phenomena being studied. As Whyte (1984:105) reminds us, "every experienced fieldworker recognizes that informants are not of equal value to the research." Representing a wide array of respondents, which we tried to do here, is important, but less so than capturing the central forces that drive offender decision-making.

Quoted material has been edited to meet the textual demands of a book of this nature. We did not, however, censor the brash, sometimes profane, language that punctuates the accounts of those we interviewed. Exposure to such language offers readers a better appreciation of the cadence of street talk and the discursive mannerisms that govern offender dialogue. At various points in the book, words or phrases in brackets will appear. These indicate an attempt on our part to explain or amplify something a respondent has said. In addition, the text is supplemented with insights from our previous field research with violent offenders to provide a more nuanced understanding of the broader social and situational context in which retaliatory acts are contemplated and carried out (cf. Mieczkowski 1986; see also Jacobs, with Wright 2000).

The book is arranged sequentially, consistent with the analytical framework used to anchor and organize the data. Chapter Two explores the retaliatory ethic and the vocabularies of motive that offenders adopt to justify its role as the preferred mode of extralegal social control. The specter of counter-retaliation, and how grievants perceive and manage this threat, are also examined. Chapter Three explores the structure, process, and contingent forms of retaliation, offering a typology to organize the data. Chapter Four considers the ways in which gender shapes the context and dynamics of retaliatory events for both men and women. Chapter Five investigates the phenomenon of "imperfect" retaliation – acts of reprisal committed against parties not responsible for the instigating affront. The reasons for imperfect retaliation and their implications for crime displacement beyond the law are specifically explored. Chapter Six addresses conceptual issues in retaliation, paying special attention to their role in the spread, intensification, and containment of urban violence. Throughout the book, and especially in the last chapter, we endeavor to be sensitive to the policy implications of our data.

# TWO

# The Retaliatory Ethic

AMERICAN SOCIETY EXPECTS urban police forces to devote their efforts to detecting and controlling street criminals. The police have responded to this expectation with intensive patrols, crackdowns, sweeps, and sophisticated covert operations – all designed to attack street criminals on their own turf. As a result, the underworld of urban street criminals is saturated with law enforcement. It is ironic, therefore, that there is probably no other setting in which recourse to the protection of the law is less available. This state of affairs is doubly ironic because urban street criminals, compared with their law-abiding counterparts, are much more vulnerable to crime.

As we noted in Chapter One, criminals are often reticent to report being victimized to the police for fear of exposing their own illicit activities. And even if they do make a police report, they are unlikely to be taken seriously because of a widespread belief among officers that lawbreakers deserve whatever fate befalls them. For all practical purposes, then, street criminals cannot really be victims in the eyes of the law; they are on their own when it comes to seeing justice done.

This implies that criminal retaliation is merely a response to the perceived unavailability of law – and to an extent this is true. But there are deeper reasons why criminal victims might choose retaliation over making an official police report, even when they might be taken seriously and could do so without risk to themselves. As this chapter will demonstrate, street criminals are enmeshed in a sub-culture in which formal law has lost its legitimacy and has come to be viewed as irrelevant to the satisfactory resolution of their day-to-day conflicts.

## Defiance and Disrespect

People are unlikely to ask the police for help in settling a dispute or resolving a grievance unless they respect police authority. Defiance of authority is part and parcel of being a street criminal. But defiance and disrespect are not equivalent. Although it is possible to defy authority without disrespecting it, street criminals do both, and this has profound implications for legal mobilization.

The decade-long War on Crime and the zero-tolerance policing that has come with it have created an atmosphere on the streets of many urban communities in which harassment and unfair treatment are perceived to be common. Time and again, the offenders we talked to complained about being stopped, searched, and interrogated for no good reason. Street offenders resent any form of official scrutiny – it increases both the direct and indirect risks of crime and makes their lives tougher in general – but *unjustified* scrutiny drew the most ire. And according to the offenders, unjustified scrutiny was more the rule than the exception. "[E]very time I have an encounter with [the police]," Crazy Jay claimed, "it's some shit that I ain't had nothing to do with." "I can't stand [the] police," insisted Lafonz. "They crooked ... pull you over for shit like not having a light over your license plate or something ... for a seatbelt [violation] ... end up running your name and searching your car ... wasn't even called for." Smoke Dog said that the police would "stop him for anything ... [walk] across a street and the light is red ... [stop me] for that." Cal called the police "shady little busters" who "ain't got nothing else better than to fuck with you. They get a hard-on fucking with another man." Neck told us that he was "scared" every time he saw the police because "you don't know what they gonna do."

Even the most hardened street offenders draw a distinction between "deserved" and "undeserved" police attention.[1] Few criminals dispute the authority of the police to patrol the streets, ask questions, conduct investigations, and make arrests. Over the years, many offenders have told us that life on the streets would be worse

---

1 Portions of the following three pages were adapted from Rosenfeld, Jacobs, and Wright (see full citation on p. 129).

without the police, a Hobbesian free-for-all where chaos and anarchy reign. But such assessments apply to policing in the abstract; the officers that the offenders actually encounter are perceived to be little better than criminals with badges who harass, intimidate, and abuse them. "[Most of my contact with the police is on] a false basis, you know," PIE complained. "They want to screw around with somebody, want to fuck with people ... The only fucking thing I had done [prior to being stopped] was being in a car with fucking people in it. [That's it] ... that's what they do. Every day." Or as Neck recalled:

> We was standing on the corner, police pulled up ... told us all to get against the wall ... We asked them, you know, what did we do, what we gotta get against the wall for? 'That ain't none of your motherfucking business! ... Just turn your ass around and get against the wall!' [T]hey searched us and shit, grabbed us, threw us against the wall ... and all this stuff. Told us to sit down on the curb and ... handcuffed us and made us sit down on the curb and told us that we weren't supposed to be on the corner ... and we wasn't doing nothing but standing ... They handcuffed us, made us sit out there in the rain for about twenty five minutes while they ran a police check on us, and then after that, when it came back clear, they come back and threaten us if they catch us on the corner again, 'We gonna lock you up,' and this and that.

Black-2 recounted a similar incident. Arriving home from the hospital with his newborn son, he discovered that his house had been burglarized. Reportedly stolen were the child's baby clothes and blankets plus the camcorder Black-2 planned to use to document his son's early years. The incident was so upsetting that, against his better judgment, Black-2 decided to call the police, who responded by arresting him for so-called self-burglary:

> [M]y house got broken into you know what I'm saying, and I had an idea who did it ... Now I called the police, I was mad. I just brought my son home. He was just born on October 30th, you know what I'm saying. November 1st I brought him

home ... [W]hen I finally came back I'm carrying my son in the kitchen and there's my mama and my grandmama hollering. When I had gone to get my child, somebody had broke in. They had put their hand through the window, came in, stole [my] weed, stole all my son's new stuff I just bought ... Clothes, little baby clothes and blankets and all that. I was mad, you know what I'm saying ... I was very upset at that and I just bought all this stuff, got my son a camcorder; they stole the camcorder. I was mad, I called the police, they locked me up. Said it looked like I had made a self-burglary ... They said 'You did the burglary. Ain't no impression of being broken into. Didn't look like something had been pushed in.' ... They like, 'You're making a self-burglary and making out somebody else took your stuff. Take the stuff and then your girl will probably go and get [new] stuff, don't let her know.' ... Accused me and locked me up. How could they lock me up for breaking into my own house? I had gone to pick up my son.

Even when offenders admit involvement in what they consider to be minor infractions, the police reportedly often blow them up into major violations. For example, during a street altercation with his girlfriend, Cora ripped off her necklace. The police, alerted by neighbors, allegedly threatened to arrest him for *robbery*:

Once, my girl and I were outside fighting, so I guess the neighbors called [the police] ... I took her chain off and broke it, so what these motherfucking police was going to do me, they were gonna lock me up for stealing or trying to put a robbery on me or something ... The motherfuckers were gonna put a robbery on me, put something hectic on me ... [it was just a fight].

Other offenders claimed that the police resorted to the use of force far too easily. Play Too Much, for instance, said that the police shot his friend in the back of the neck as he attempted to flee, killing him. Duff reported that the police had maced, handcuffed, and beaten his cousin with a flashlight at a family reunion, though the cousin had done nothing to antagonize them. D-Boy told us that the police had nearly assaulted and maced his brother during an "extraction" that should have been peaceable. Such incidents, according to D-Boy, fuel the contempt that many inner-city residents have for law enforcement. That contempt sometimes results in violent resistance:

> They pointing at him trying to provoke him and he like, 'Okay, man, let me just get my stuff.' They like got the mace. They just want to do something to him, want to beat his ass, want to knock him out with some mace and they provoking him. The one guy [police officer] kept touching him. And I say, 'Officer, he's getting his stuff. There's no need for you to put your hands on him' and his buddy recognized that I knew something about something ... The officer tells me, 'You get the fuck back in the house.' 'Now listen, she [my aunt] called you to come serve us and yet you come to our house telling us to get the fuck back in the house. I don't understand, man.' And then they wonder why they get shot at and shit ... [A] lot of the police ain't right, man, theyself.

## Incompetent Policing

If contempt for the police is the primary reason that street criminals seldom seek their help, a widespread belief in their incompetence must run a close second. It can be argued that even the strongest enmity for official authority might give way to grudging respect if the police were perceived as sufficiently adept at identifying violators and bringing them to justice. But this is not the case on the streets of urban America, where the police are seen to be indolent, loathe to expend the time and effort required to follow through on leads, and apathetic about pursuing real justice.

The police are rarely around when violations occur anyway, making it perceptibly pointless to call them even if legal mobilization was considered a legitimate option. "What are the cops gonna do?" Play Too Much asked rhetorically. "It's gonna take them five or ten minutes to get there ... [W]hoever did it [robbed me] ... gonna be gone and went on ... I mean come on, man ... I could have been out there doing my own police work so to speak ... I'll get those people before they will." "Those mother-fuckers ain't gonna do nothing," Jay chimed in. "They'll take our statements and send us on our way home." "Police don't do noth-ing," M-1 complained. "If you tell the police some minor stuff like that [being robbed of $50], they be like, 'Okay,' but ain't nothin gonna happen ... they tell you they gonna investigate but man [they don't] ... Shit, somebody stole my car and the police honestly told me [they] weren't lookin' for it. 'We got too many cars out there [already].'"

D-Boy alerted the police for help in finding his stolen car. He provided a detailed description and waited for a resolution, only to locate the vehicle himself a few days later, parked in an area the police routinely patrol. "'What's the deal man?,'" he recalled asking one officer. "'It was right down the street. You ride through here all day long.' 'We don't want to fucking hear that shit' [the officer said], but yet on the car it says what? To protect and ser-ve ... most of the time there's no service ... they really don't give a fuck." Hops suggested cowardice was just as much to blame for this state of affairs as laziness, claiming that the police were afraid to intervene in so-called street beefs. They "can't really squash no street beef, for real ... They ain't gonna jeopardize theyself like that. They gonna get out of the way."

## Ineffectual Law

The perceived weakness of official sanctions also discourages offenders from seeking legal redress of their grievances. The law may be tough in theory but, according to the offenders, its practical application is substantially less intimidating. This view may seem ironic coming, as it does, from street criminals until you recognize their "punitive definition of justice" (Markowitz and Felson 1998; Peterson 1999) and the degree to which it shapes their interpretation of projected consequences. For individuals who measure justice by the infliction of pain, the marginal loss of liberty does not qualify as sufficient punishment, at least not for anyone other than themselves. "What are they gonna get [for shooting my uncle]?," Moon asked.

"In a year he'll be out. That ain't enough." Lady Ice insisted that the women who assaulted her with a baseball bat would get no time. "[I committed] assaults before," she recalled, "and I didn't get no time ... They just give you your [probation] papers and put it on your record and that's it ... That's all they gonna do."

Formal sanctions are not only deemed by offenders to be weak, they also are widely regarded as separate from informal ones; experiencing the former has little to do with facing the latter. At least two respondents explicitly preferred that the individuals who crossed them *not* go to jail because un-incarcerated wrongdoers were easier to hunt down and pay back. "That [arrest and jail time] don't mean shit." Black underscored. "That's on him if he got caught up." Moon made it clear that even if the man who shot his uncle in the stomach with a .38 ended up serving time, it would not lessen his desire to retaliate. "He still owes us, man, he still owes us. Owes us for real." Down Low's brother reportedly retaliated against a drug rival twenty one years after the man had shot him; the rival had spent the first eighteen of those twenty one years in prison. Player suggested that the authorities could not give "enough time" to the man who assaulted his sister during a domestic dispute, breaking her nose and blinding her in one eye. "I'm still gonna fuck him up when ever I see him ... I'm gonna put a pussy in his head whenever I see him and I'm not going to go up and try to punch this motherfucker. I'm gonna put a pipe on his motherfucking ass." Comments by Block and M-1 encapsulate the logic of retaliatory justice:

> Police can't do nothing but [take someone] to jail. That's all he gonna do is go to jail. I rob a nigger dead and whatever, just like what he did to my people. He kill my people, I want him dead ... [I]f he whip my people, we're going to whip him. If he shoot at my people, we gonna shoot at him. [Block]

> They [the men who robbed me] took out a gun to your face, cuss you out ... kickin' you ... while you're on the ground ... disrespect you ... [calling me names like] bitch ass ... took your money, took your pocket weed, took [my partner's] money ...

[Jail is not enough because] I feel like I'm not the one doing the punishment to him ... they [the authorities] giving him the punishment. I want him to face the punishment for what he did to me ... I want my money. I want interest. [M-1]

## Disrespect and Deterrence

The powerful emphasis that offenders place on personal justice derives from the cultural ethos of the street corner, in which self-reliance is paramount and maintaining a reputation for toughness dominates day-to-day interaction (Anderson 1999). Word about what individuals do or fail to do in response to a violation committed against them travels fast. Responses, good or bad, give rise to an informal but powerful status hierarchy that mediates how people perceive, judge, and treat you. A decisive counter-strike projects an image of someone not to be crossed, helping to insulate you from future predation. Perceived weakness, conversely, invites only further exploitation (Topalli, Wright, and Fornango 2002).

On the street corner, no affront is trivial. How you react to even the smallest affront says a lot about how you will react to a major one. Letting something minor "slide" can signal weakness, and a reputation for weakness is an open invitation for others to take advantage of you, to treat you like a so-called "punk" or "bitch." "Motherfuckers around [here] will try you two, three times a day," Black explained. "They don't give a fuck ... If one motherfucker bitch you, everybody's gonna bitch you ... smack on you, steal on you, whatever ...." TD concurred: "If I let [something] slide, you might try to come at me the same day or the next day because you think, 'Aw he's a punk, he let it slide, he can't handle it like a man' ...." Similarly, Hops claimed that "you gotta put your foot down and let them know ... it ain't even happening so don't even come this way ...." And Sugar concluded: "[If I don't retaliate, anybody] can just walk up and take my shit. Come and punch me and take my dope and take my motherfucking weed, they'll be thinking I ain't shit. I ain't standing up on mine."

The retaliatory ethic therefore reflects not just a desire to punish, but also a perceived need to deter future aggression. According to the offenders we interviewed, ensuring that this dual objective is accomplished successfully demands that retaliatory responses be more severe, intense, and punitive than the instigating affront. "[W]hen you get they ass, give them harder than what they gave you," Sugar insisted, "make the motherfucker think twice not to fuck with you no more." "I'm coming back harder and I'm coming back even a little bit stronger," warned Red. "[I'm] cutting it off before it becomes worse."

Extreme reactions to seemingly minor transgressions betray the street criminals' abiding faith in punitive excess. Red, for example, shot a man after he slapped him for accidentally spilling a glass of cognac on his clothing. Likewise, Mad Dog, a crack dealer, broke a male customer's finger by snapping it back during a handshake because he had reneged on a $20 drug debt. And Pumpkin beat a woman senseless after she called the police on her brother for domestic abuse. In street culture, the severity of the affront is less important than the affront itself (Baron, Forde, and Kennedy 2001). That said, particularly serious affronts tend to elicit the most severe responses of all, as Sugar and Crazy Jay – robbed and carjacked, respectively – attest:

My partner had a big stick. She was hitting [the woman who robbed us] like in her ribs. And I was just hitting her, I had her hair anyway. I was just hitting her in her face and my friend had a stick and we stood over her and was stomping her ass. All of her face must sag just kicking her ass, just whooping her ass ....'You taking my motherfucker shit. You ain't gonna do that shit no more. I ain't the bitch to play with.' We was whooping her ass ... then she balled up in a knot and I got her for one last time. [Sugar]

[I] started hitting him [the carjacker] with the gun ... 30 or 40 times ... on top of his head, on his back, on his face ....'You puss ass nigger,' [I said], 'you bitch ass nigger, you motherfucking dope head' ... just stomping on him, getting in his motherfucker

33

face ... he was as bloody as a motherfucker ... after I hit him so many times I was starting to lose my breath so I stood back ... and I didn't feel no sympathy for him ... Was his bones gonna ever heal? Was his motherfucking scabs gonna clear? I didn't think about none of that shit, fuck that ... he didn't think about how my [infant] son is doing [when he carjacked me], he ain't thinking about goddamn me, who was gonna put pads [diapers] on my son now. He didn't think about was I gonna be able to pay my rent, you know what I'm saying, so I ain't think about none of his shit. [Crazy Jay]

The prominence of physical punishment in the street criminals' preferred retaliatory repertoire is noteworthy because the universe of possible responses includes numerous other options. If revenge is a "banquet table full of luscious possibilities" (Barreca 1995:35), why does violence figure so prominently in the offenders' accounts? It may be that the offenders want violators, literally, to feel the bite of justice. Breaking into violators' homes or vandalizing their property may hurt them, but not in the visceral way many offenders desire. Moreover, mediated punishment – that is, punishment inflicted indirectly through an object – risks making the offender look weak, as if they're too afraid or intimidated to confront the violator in person. Property crime is certainly a retributive option, as we shall see in Chapter Three, but on the street corner, direct confrontation is generally the preferred response:

I want to touch him [the violator]. I didn't want to touch nothing of his. You know I wanted to touch him. Let him know what I'm feeling, you know, I couldn't, I couldn't just take it out. That bitch shit to just go back and beat up his car or bust his windows out and all that shit. That's whore shit. [Biddle]

### The Pedagogy of Violent Retaliation

There is nothing subtle about violence – that is part of its appeal for retribution-minded street criminals. For those unaccustomed to reasoned debate, violence can be profoundly pedagogical. "The thing about retaliation," Mad Dog intoned, "is to teach them a lesson. Whatever was did, don't do it because you're going to get hurt." Crazy Jay put it this way: "[I]f the thought ever cross your mind about trying to fuck with me, let this [beating] ... pop in your head ... if you ever, ever, ever decide to do that shit again, think about this first cause it gonna be even more severe." Some offenders engage in "trash talk" when getting even, to let the wrongdoer know in no uncertain terms who is in control.

> I got your punk ass and now look at you ... Now if you'd have paid this cheese [money back to me], you'd have been all right, but now you fucked up, you bleeding and shit ... you talking about your ribs broke. Now what the fuck? [Bobcat]
>
> Punk ass nigger ... earlier you was 'fuck me. I ain't shit. I'm soft' ... what's up now?' [Smoke Dog]
>
> I'm getting you for taking my motherfucking shit. I'm beating your ass. You're gonna give me your shitting ass. [Sugar]

In other settings, language may act as a proxy for physical force. In street culture, however, words are less a substitute for blows than they are a way to amplify their pain. Street offenders often relish the opportunity to mete out their own brand of justice. Marginalized in virtually every other aspect of their lives, offenders find that the chance to deliver justice *personally* opens up a source of existential power available to them almost nowhere else. Catching and punishing those who have wronged them makes offenders feel mighty, while at the same time it masks their objective impotence. "I love retaliation," Sugar beamed. "I love to see the motherfuckers down like they did me." "I had an adrenaline rush," recalled Pumpkin after beating the woman who called the police on her brother, "like I was the shit, like I was in control." "I [felt] strong," Mad Dog explained, "I [felt] excited ... finally, I got my point across. They know not to fuck with me." Biddle described the seductive satisfaction of getting even in sexual terms. "I felt just like I was in some pussy," he recalled after using a baseball bat to break the legs of the man who vandalized his car. "You know [like I] busted [a] nut [ejaculated]."

Imperfect retaliation – that is, revenge exacted from someone other than the person directly responsible for the instigating violation – does not appear to offer as much satisfaction, and is therefore not a preferred MO. This is significant inasmuch as even imperfect strikes may allow offenders to recoup losses or vent their anger. But in these cases, the culpable violator remains unpunished, so real justice has not been achieved. This is to say nothing about the issue of conscience. Although moral qualms do not figure prominently in the psyches of most street offenders, even criminals may have misgivings about exacting retribution from an uninvolved third party.

None of this is to suggest that displaced retaliation plays no role in the retaliatory repertoire of street offenders. It does, especially when losses must be recouped in a hurry and the real violator cannot be located. But displaced retaliation is almost invariably the option of last resort. Chapter Five explores the logic, structure, and process of displaced retaliation in greater detail.

## Counter-retaliation

For street offenders, the most dissonance-inducing aspect of retaliation is the widespread recognition that it can backfire and trigger counter-retaliation. Punishment that is perceived to be excessive is especially likely to be interpreted by the original violator as a fresh affront that must be avenged. Victims and violators appear to swap places, setting the stage for an escalating cycle of violence. As Baumeister and Campbell (1999:211) put it: "Just when one side may regard the score as settled, because in its view the other's suffering matches its own, the other side is likely to see a huge imbalance calling for [predatory] redress."

Conflict spirals result mainly from the fact that the "arithmetics" of punishment differ for victims and violators, with the former perceiving transgressions to be far more serious than do the latter. This calculus holds regardless of whether strikes are committed in the name of retaliation or counter-retaliation. "Such different arithmetics ... occur because of an egocentric bias in the experience of pain ... and/or because some harms are hard to quantify, as when 'the principle of the thing' is at stake" (Bies and Tripp 1996:259). In other words, violators may perceive an initial attack to be "not that bad," while victims feel intensely wronged, and strike back accordingly. The original violators, in turn, interpret this counter-strike as excessive and thus set out to "get even." Paradoxically, each side in such conflicts often believes that its actions are defensive in nature (see Bies and Tripp 2001:203).

A defining characteristic of hardened street criminal-grievants is the extent to which they recognize the risk of counter-reprisal and retaliate in spite of it. Central to this attitude is an abiding sense of fatalism – the singular belief that whatever is going to happen is going to happen, so why worry about it. Fatalism is based on the notion that worrying absorbs valuable cognitive energy that might be better spent on more immediate concerns, and it does so at the expense of something over which you have little control.

The ability of street offenders to discount worry about the future is especially important given that the most prominent dilemma of counter-retaliation is its uncertainty (for a discussion of ontological security and vulnerability in a street culture setting, see Topalli, Wright, and Fornango 2002). Street offenders typically commit a considerable amount of "dirt" irrespective of any particular retaliatory strike. Although St. Louis is a fair-sized city, the environs within which its criminal population circulates are limited – victims and victimizers inevitably cross paths, and as a result their world is fraught with danger. Fatalism offers a way to cope with that danger, at least cognitively:

> There's so much shit [I] done, man. You just can't be worried at all ... when it catches up with you, you gotta face that shit. So you know I ain't tripping on that ... It's not a worry thing, cause I really accept whatever ... cause when you put down a lot of bullshit like I have, you got to accept this ... Don't think I'm looking forward to it, but if it ever happens, [it happens] [Player]

You get used to it after a while. You can't go around being worried about shit like that. It'd just fuck your head up … Worrying about having to, you know, watching over your shoulder all the time, worried about if I see this dude am I gonna have to do this? Is this dude looking for me, you know. If I leave the house without my gun should I do that cause I know these two [violators I retaliated against] might come after me. I mean, there's probably more people that want to beat my ass than these two … guys. So you just get used to it after a while. [Lafonz]

I do so much dirt to the point that one day my time is gonna come and that's just not in my mind worrying at all … I don't change [any of my habits]. I still go to the same places, hang out with the same people … ride the same block … ride the same car … Once you just get to that point you're not scared of nothing, then dying, you really ain't scared of that at all. [Goldie]

Fatalism does more than reduce the potency of fear; it also frees street offenders to focus their attention on aspects of their physical and social environment that signal threat and demand action. When the psyche is not overwhelmed with anxiety, danger signs are easier to spot. The capacity for fatalism to enhance rationality in this way has not, to our knowledge, been explored by contemporary social scientists, but it has clear strategic value in a context where would-be assailants are prepared to use their guile to lull intended victims into a false sense of security. It reportedly is common, for example, for a rival to send a signal that, as far as he is concerned, a dispute is over as a way of getting potential victims to lower their guard. "That's the way people be getting other people," Chewy explained. "I think it's a punk move." Punk move or not, there are no rules in street disputes, only winners and losers, so anything that confers an advantage over an antagonist is perceived to be fair. As a result, both those who strike and those who strike back cannot take things at face value and must constantly be on their guard to avoid becoming complacent:

[O]ne of my cousins is still cool with [the violator] … every time I call my cousin she was like, 'Oh she's [the violator] still looking for you' or 'She say when she finally get in touch with you, she gonna do this and do that' ... then all of a sudden ... [I'll hear about how the violator is] talking about how [she] don't see how I let our friendship mess up and all that other stuff ... basically trying to make a thing like she's trying to be friendly, but nine times out of ten she's not ... Basically to get me to come down there ... to beat me up. [Stacy]

He [the violator] told a friend of mine that he wanted to squash it. He's like, 'Man, I gotta talk to him cause he is tripping, dog' ... I'm like, man, fuck them, man ... I say that nigger bullshitting. That's just something to keep that motherfucker up, keep a little heat off. [Hops]

Obviously there is little need to remain on guard for offenders who take steps to eliminate the possibility of future counter-strikes (see Jacobs, Topalli, and Wright 2000). Though most of our respondents used force to deter counter-retaliation, Red – one of the most ruthless members of the sample – did so to prevent it altogether.

Red:          [W]hy whoop his ass and then that's another problem? ... When I say that's another problem, the problem is that you should have went on and killed him [when you retaliated] because, you dig, now you got to make sure whenever you ride around in the neighborhood, you dig, he might run up on you and shoot you in your car. Or he might ride up beside you and shoot you .... You might be going today. You might like, 'Why, I should have gone on and killed this nigger when I had him.' You know?

Interviewer:  Yeah. Because he's not thinking about the fact that you spared him [during the retaliatory strike].

Red:          Right.

Interviewer:  He's thinking about the fact that you beat him up.

Red:          Right. And then that's retaliation. You know, you see that's [counter] retaliation coming down on the thing there.

As already noted, however, most of the criminal victims we interviewed were unwilling to go to such lengths because doing so carried risks of its own. Bodies can bring "heat" from the police but, more importantly, retaliatory proxies may well take up the dead violator's cause. Red confirmed this, telling us that the brother of one of his victims once confronted him in a metropark, saying he was going to kill him. Armed at the time, Red was able to face down the aggressor and make an escape. "I told him to come on with it," Red recalled. "While he's talking, I'm already strapped ... I'm reaching for mine [gun under the car seat] ... he gets bagged up [he leaves] cause he knew I was strapped. At this time he wasn't strapped." Three months later, Red ran into the same man outside a movie theater. An angry verbal exchange ensued, but the presence of a security guard deterred any physical violence. Several weeks afterward, the two antagonists ran into one another once again in a drugstore parking lot, and a pitched gun battle broke out. Red escaped uninjured.

Sugar was less fortunate. Three months after assaulting and robbing a woman who had robbed her, she was kidnapped, beaten severely, and robbed of over a kilogram of crack by the victim and an accomplice. Her assailants forced her to reveal the location of several of her drug-dealing associates in order to end the assault and to prevent others "really close" to her from being hurt. Her associates were then methodically robbed:

> I was going to the store. Her and her partner surrounded the store. I went into the store and they caught me. They blindfolded me this time. Put my hands behind around my back and duct-taped me. Put me in the [car], robbed me, and they whooped my ass. They whooped my ass bad ... stole all my money and I had to tell on my other partner[s] because they said they would kill all those people close to me if I wasn't gonna tell, so I went ahead and told and they robbed my partner[s] .... They robbed about six of them ... that night. They all caught them one by one.

As this case illustrates, retaliatory cycles can sometimes widen to include innocent third parties. Indeed, vengeance's most troubling feature may be its capacity to extend beyond the boundaries of the initial dispute and to spin out of control, generating more and more violence in the process.

## The Mechanics of Retaliation

Street criminals can seldom stake a legitimate claim to victim status, and therefore must assume principle responsibility for righting perceived wrongs. This precipitates decentralized social control and corrective action in the form of street justice. Vigilantism is enhanced by strong cultural prescriptions that encourage street criminals to display fearsome toughness in the face of threat and openly defy official authority. Retaliation accomplishes both.

Observers often assume that violence is the "very embodiment of evil" (Cooney 1998:3), but much of it is committed *not* for material gain or pleasure or anything analogous (though those benefits may be incidental), but rather for moralistic reasons – to right a perceived wrong (Black 1983). The nature of the instigating affront is not necessarily important in the commission of such acts, especially in honor cultures like the underworld of street criminals. Here, the trigger for retaliatory aggression is sensitivity to slights. Though it is ironic that this hypersensitivity flourishes in an essentially lawless setting, it is precisely the outlaw context of these interpersonal encounters that requires things to be so cut-and-dried.

Retaliation is often thought to be carried out with the norm of reciprocity in mind – that is, with a view to restoring balance by "getting even." But retaliation is about more than that. Retaliatory strikes often exceed the original affront in intensity and severity, both because they have a strongly punitive – or "expressive" – character and because they are designed to deter future aggression. For reprisal to work in these two ways, it has to have "bite." The bite of street justice is the point at which punishment and deterrence intersect. If the bite is not sufficiently deep, deterrence is compromised by asymmetries between the instigating affront and the resulting punishment. For those who lack access to the formal machinery of dispute resolution, the cost of being perceived as too lenient is a greater risk of future victimization.

Again, there is more at stake here than continuing vulnerability. On the street, personal affronts attack identity and not simply some political or economic utility (Miller 2001; Gabriel 1998; Greenberg

1993). Counter-strikes in defense of identity tend to be excessive, especially in settings where even minor slights are interpreted as major blows to character. Lacking access to the occupational and familial roles through which status traditionally is conferred, street offenders rely instead on the honor that accrues to those who demonstrate prowess in disputes. On the street corner, honor is accumulated much like real capital (Marongiu and Newman 1987:98), and bringing someone down for what he did to you, raises your personal market worth in the eyes of your peers.

Ironically, the more punitive the retaliatory strike, the more likely it is that recipients will conclude that they too have been wronged. The tendency for street offenders to want to show up those who victimize them as "punks" means that their attempts to "get even" will often be perceived as brand-new affronts crying out for redress. Retaliation that generates defiance rather than deterrence has obviously backfired. But worrying about counter-strikes is unwise because it can forestall decisive action and put grievants at risk of appearing weak. Perceived weakness may not only trigger additional attacks, it also may lead to a loss of status and respect. Thus, criminal victims would rather retaliate hard and face the *potential* consequences than jeopardize their reputations as people not to be messed with through inaction.

It is unlikely that criminal victims would alert the police even if access to the law were realistically available to them; asking for help makes it apparent that one cannot handle his or her own business. And in the absence of a demonstrated ability to fight back, those who approach the authorities for assistance increase the possibility that the accused will seek revenge at some point in the future. In the context of street life, this risk is amplified many fold by virtue of the setting's inherent lawlessness.

Whether – and, if so, how – *violators* employ formal social control to protect themselves against retaliation is a separate and more intriguing question. At least in theory, violators in the cross-hairs of an imminent retaliatory strike could decide to *increase* their exposure to formal sanctions by getting caught on purpose. The extent to which disputants employ the police as a resource to avoid retaliatory consequences has not been explored in any detail by contemporary criminologists. Indeed, the degree to which offenders mobilize formal authorities in any capacity has historically received little criminological attention. Perhaps the closest analogue is "snitching," the process by which criminals give information to the police in exchange for material reward or reduced punishment. But snitching typically occurs under duress, so it really constitutes legal mobilization in reverse (Rosenfeld, Jacobs, and Wright 2003).

Purposely exposing yourself to arrest and incarceration might appear extreme but, done well, it could offer protection from retaliation with no imputation of fear or weakness. The police, after all, are the ones doing the removing, and few would suspect offenders of purposely engineering their own apprehension. How long the cooling out period has to last before things "settle down" is a separate question, as is the extent to which retaliation follows offenders from the streets into prison. Given the constant flow of criminals into and out of jail, the chances of running into a family member or associate of the grievant must be substantial, so retaliation by proxy is a real possibility. Violators may be safer in prison, but they are never entirely secure. And if anger festers after an affront, instead of simmering down, the threat of retaliation may build rather than dissipate over time. Chapter Three explores the implications of delayed retaliation for the spread of urban violence in greater detail.

# THREE

# A Typology of Criminal Retaliation

IN THE BEST OF ALL POSSIBLE WORLDS, most street criminals want to strike back at those who cross them immediately. Not doing so risks being labeled a punk, and no excuse can deflect the stigma that invariably accompanies unjustified surrender. A reflexive reaction is especially important when audiences are present because, on the street, third parties are the final arbiters of status (Wilkinson and Fagan 2001:174). Word travels fast, and the reputational damage flowing from any appearance of cowardice can be serious and long-lasting.

But street criminals do not inhabit the best of all possible worlds; their milieu is filled with uncertainty, and they are not always able to exact payback quickly. The affront committed against them may not involve face-to-face contact. And even if it does involve such contact, the violator may get away before they can strike back. Perhaps they did not know the person who wronged them. Information about the violator's identity or whereabouts might not emerge until well after an affront, if it emerges at all. Once that happens, they still may have to wait to catch the violator in a sufficiently compromising position before retaliating. They might not be able to generate enough coercive power, or they may be in a setting unsuited to revenge. They may want to retaliate then and there, but face costs and risks (for example, foregone criminal opportunities, chances of injury or arrest) that are too high to justify an immediate strike.

Criminals who prey on other criminals know that they risk retaliation, and they employ various techniques in an attempt to eliminate or delay that possibility. They may target people who do not know them; they may wear a disguise to hide their identity; they

45

may lay low and/or exercise mobility to make it difficult to find them; and they almost invariably maintain a high degree of vigilance and defensibility to head off a retaliatory strike if and when it comes (see Jacobs, Topalli, and Wright 2000). The result is that desiring to retaliate immediately is not the same thing as doing so. For all the lip service that street criminals pay to the critical importance of quickly striking back at those who cross them, prevailing situational factors often make it hard for them to practice what they preach.

The delays and uncertainty that surround the pressing desire to retaliate are especially significant because affronts attack ontological security rather than some economic or political utility (Miller 2001; Gabriel 1998; Greenberg 1993). It is precisely because injustice threatens the security of identity that wronged parties find it so disturbing. This is especially true in street culture, where even minor violations can assume major importance. Strikes that are delayed or that do not involve face-to-face contact threaten damage beyond that created by the violation itself. Thus, the ways in which wronged parties employ retaliatory modalities to restore and enhance both identity and security are of vital interest.

These modalities can take one of six forms. Immediate reprisal that involves face-to-face contact with the violator is called "reflexive" retaliation. Immediate reprisal that involves no face-to-face contact is called "reflexively displaced" retaliation.[1] When retaliation is delayed, an added contingency is introduced – whether or not the delay is desired by the retaliating party. This permits four additional possibilities. Face-to-face retaliation where delay is desired is called "calculated" retaliation. Face-to-face retaliation where delay is *not* desired is called "deferred" retaliation. Retaliation without face-to-face contact where delay is desired is called "sneaky" retaliation. Retaliation without face-to-face contact where delay is *not* desired is called "imperfect" retaliation. For the sake of clarity, these different forms of retaliation are presented as distinct entities; in practice, however, they often fade from one form to another with the passage of time.

---

[1] There were no reported cases of reflexively displaced retaliation, so this category necessarily is residual. The reasons for its absence will be explored in greater detail later.

## Reflexive Retaliation

"Reflexive retaliation" is face-to-face retribution exacted immediately after an affront takes place. It represents a knee-jerk response to the perceived violation, something inextricably tied to the offending moment. Of all of the various forms of retaliation, this one best fits the commonsense understanding of what street justice is all about. Somebody wrongs you, and you wrong that person right back, immediately, without hesitation. Cognition moves rapidly from "cold" to "hot," as decisions flow directly into action (Wilkinson and Fagan 2001:190). Reflexive strikes require that the initial affront involve face-to-face contact. Without such contact, the aggrieved party has to track the responsible party down before retaliating, and this inevitably creates delay.

Reflexive retaliation is an outgrowth of the imperatives of street culture, imperatives that place great emphasis on spontaneous action and instant gratification (see Shover 1996). Waiting before striking back against an aggressor can also make you look afraid, and fear is anathema on the street corner. Lashing out is much better. Intolerance earns respect and makes you look strong. Strength is protective.

Chewy thus beat a man into submission because he chastised him for engaging a woman in street conversation – ostensibly for the purpose of "picking her up." The man claimed that the woman was his wife, but it turned out that they were not married. This claim, in and of itself, did not provoke Chewy's ire, rather it was the man's tenor and language that moved him to take action:

> He started talking noise ... calling me a punk and stuff ... weak ... I just upped on him ... I hit him a couple of times and then I grabbed him, threw him on the ground and was on top of his hand. I busted it up. Then I started hitting him in his chest, you know, punking him.

J Hustle used a crow bar to beat a man who verbally disrespected him. The violator was the cousin of someone who had defrauded him in a petty cell phone scam. That scam was minor enough that

47

J Hustle had been prepared to let it slide until, that is, the cousin began rubbing his face in it:

> [H]is cousin comes around bragging ... 'He took your mother-fucking money.' .... I'm like man, you get out of my face, you know. He just kept on talking shit about me not getting my money and I just happened to have like a little crow bar in my hand. Think I had it in case somebody try to steal my car or something. He just kept pushing me and pushing me and pushing me. I wasn't gonna do nothing to him, and I just hit him across his face with the crow bar.

When the affront involves physical violence, a quick and forceful reaction becomes even more important. If insults and disrespectful comments can call you into question, physical attacks remove all doubt that the assailant does not perceive you as sufficiently intimidating. The only viable response is to strike back forcefully. Black, for example, was hit on the head after making disparaging sexual remarks about the assailant's sister. The blow occurred from behind – rendering it, in Black's words, "cowardly shit." Black responded with a punch. A fight ensued, but Black was unable to deliver the severe punishment he felt was justified by the circumstances. He struck again two days later, this time in more calculated fashion (described in "Calculated Retaliation" shortly). Though Black committed the initial violation in this case, the point is that street disputes often escalate. With no formal body prepared to intervene, such conflicts tend to build sequentially, with retaliation breeding counter-retaliation in an uncontrolled spiral of violence (see, for example, Luckenbill 1977; Meier, Kennedy, and Sacco 2001; Wolfgang 1958).

Not only do street disputes frequently escalate, they also have a tendency to draw uninvolved others into them. Such was the case with Lafonz, who found himself embroiled in conflict during a neighborhood basketball game. A man called a foul on one of Lafonz's friends, who in turn complained that the call was picky. An angry exchange of words followed, drawing in another one of Lafonz's friends. A fight erupted, but it quickly became apparent that the pair was outmatched. Accordingly, Lafonz jumped into the fight to help them out. Although on the surface this act might appear to be altruistic, it clearly was rooted in self-interest. Had Lafonz failed to provide back-up, word that he had pulled a "bitch move" would quickly have gotten back to the neighborhood, thereby sullying his reputation:

> Because we all friends, you know what I'm saying? It's like I can't let you get beat up and just sit there and watch it. ... It'd just be ... that'd be a bitch move ... it'd have made me look bad ... we from the same neighborhood and if I sit there and let these two grown-ass men beat these two little dude's ass that's gonna look bad on me.

Given the undoubted importance of immediate retaliation in the calculus of street justice, it is perhaps especially important to explain those situations in which reflexive strikes do *not* occur. Our data suggest that this happens for one of three reasons: (1) the opportunity to strike reflexively is absent; (2) the situational context makes doing so illogical; or (3) the wronged party *wants* to wait before retaliating for strategic reasons. Primary among these reasons is to cultivate the element of surprise.

## Calculated Retaliation

"Calculated retaliation" is face-to-face, delayed retribution where the delay is intentional. Typically, delays are an outgrowth of the wronged party's attempt to secure a competitive advantage over the violator. They want violators to believe that they have "moved on" by forgiving or forgetting the affront. This is done to cultivate the element of surprise.

Convincing opponents to lower their guard is perhaps the best strategy for gaining the upper hand in all predatory encounters – retaliatory or otherwise. Stalking violators openly, or letting them know that you are still angry, tips your hand and perhaps allows them to mount a preemptive strike. Waiting also permits you to

49

eliminate any competitive advantage the violator might otherwise have, while allowing you to retaliate in a form and at a level of your choosing.

Recall Black's dissatisfaction with his initial reflexive strike against the associate who punched him from behind. "I didn't get no solid lick of his ass [that night]," he complained. "I didn't get mine back." Biding his time for a couple of days in an attempt to convince the violator that "everything was cool," Black struck with full force when he felt the moment was opportune. Importantly, he exacted his retribution in front of an audience, perhaps to "show up" his assailant in the same way that he himself had been shown up. Black also appeared to use the onlookers as a lure to bring the violator out and make him feel comfortable, as is evident next:

> He walked down the steps ... in front of his house ... just standing there. You know, we in a group, we down the street. We just talking. I figure that as he walk down the steps. I just didn't approach him then. He started coming down where the crowd was ... it was cool ... when he got down there that was it. ... I just did to him what he did to me ....I hit his motherfucking ass. ... I just hauled off and stole his ass. ... [Then] I kicked him and kicked him ... he was gone.

Similarly, Hops recounted a calculated strike initiated in the wake of an insufficiently punitive reflexive one. The angry ex-boyfriend of the woman Hops was seeing unexpectedly showed up at the woman's home. The boyfriend, seeing Hops and the woman together, became enraged – grabbing Hops by the neck and tussling with him. The fracas was brief, and the ex-boyfriend walked out the door unscathed. Dissatisfied, Hops went after him. "I just said 'fuck it!' and just went out front ... He was going ... toward his car and I just ran off, ran toward him ... jumped on his back, grabbed him by the neck, chopping him down to the ground, punching him and beating him ... fucked him up." An hour and a half later, the ex-boyfriend came back armed with weapons and friends, but Hops had already left the house. The dispute remained in a state of incubation at the time of our interview, but it seems destined to be reawakened at some point in the future – a view confirmed by Hops, who told us: "[W]e've been on ever since."

Sugar, robbed while she was selling drugs, managed to yank off the perpetrator's mask. In doing so, she recognized the robber as another female drug dealer who apparently had become jealous of her success. Rather than retaliating immediately, Sugar decided to wait "a week and let it die down a minute ... [to] let [that] whore ... think [she] got me." Driving down the street one evening, Sugar and an accomplice spotted the woman who robbed her at a bus stop. They followed the bus until the woman got off and attacked her as she walked home. With the help of her accomplice, Sugar beat the woman mercilessly and managed to recoup far more than the $350 cash and quarter pound of marijuana that had been taken in the robbery:

> My partner had a big stick. She was hitting her like in her ribs. ... I was just hitting her in her face ... stomping her ass ... whipping her ass ... big old cut ... right back here by her ear ... face all fucked up ... and then I got like directly in front of her and I kind of like stomped her down in a sack ... 'You taking my motherfucker shit. You ain't gonna do that shit no more. I ain't the bitch to play with' ....[We took a] thousand dollars ... two quarter pounds [of marijuana] ... big [diamond rings] ... nice little chain ... earrings. ... We took every motherfucking thing.

In a separate incident, Sugar herself was robbed and assaulted at a bus stop by another rival drug dealer. Injured badly during the attack, she was forced to lay low for three weeks to recover. After recuperating, she waited another three weeks to maximize the shock value of her counter-attack. Stalking the drug dealer who had robbed her, Sugar hid in the alley and struck when the woman returned to retrieve her drug stash. She ended up shooting the woman, though she insisted that her initial intention was only to rob her. One of the drug dealer's friends intervened with a machete, forcing Sugar's hand: [I]t took my eyes like three weeks to clear up [from the assault], but I gave it a little bit more time than that. I gave it like

about a month and a half. ... Because I wanted her to keep thinking, cause she figured by this time if I hadn't come back to get her
then I wouldn't come back to get her, but I was and I was so mad on
the fact that she blacked [my] eyes and they were bloodshot and you
got the neighborhood all coming to me all like I'm a punk or
something. ... I was heated. So I got a couple of my partners
up ... and we let it get dark cause they always be on the set, sitting
down in front of a car drinking and smoking weed and stuff like this
so we waited. She's a popper, you know, she pop crack. She don't
smoke it, she sell it ... We came back around and we parked at the
top of the street ... [people] was pointing us to the girl down the
street, letting us know [where she was] ... I had got a little .45. My
partner went across the street, walked on the other side, and I
walked on this side. She came and we just stood there and watched
until she came to the back and I upped it [my gun] on her, and I
showed my face and said, 'You remember me? You took all my
shit.' ... 'Bitch, I want my shit! Then I'm gonna take your
shit.' ... And I had put my gun like in the corner of her mouth ... I
guess one of her partners heard a little squabble going on back there.
They came back and she had a machete on her the other time; that's
how I end up popping the girl in her legs ... She's sitting in a
wheelchair now.[2]

Street criminals who are victimized by other offenders need not
wait long to exact revenge. Indeed, it behooves them not to delay,
lest it appear that they lack the backbone to retaliate. How long
grievants wait is less important than the way in which they balance
time and space to cultivate the element of surprise. Crazy Jay, for
example, was robbed at gunpoint of $600 cash, his car, and a ring
he had purchased for his infant son. The robber was wearing a
mask, but Crazy Jay recognized his voice and work boots, which
had distinctive paint stains. The robber was a crack user who lived
in the same extended-stay motel that Crazy Jay stayed at, and who
had bought drugs from him on numerous occasions in the past.

[2] As is evident from anecdotes like this one, grievants and violators are often difficult to
distinguish.

Setting his alarm for 7:00 AM the following morning, Crazy Jay and an associate burst into the robber's apartment and "shocked his ass," beating him senseless:

> [I] started hitting him with the gun ... 30 or 40 times ... on top of his head, on his back, on his face ... after I hit him so many times I was starting to lose my breath so I stood back ... I cocked my gun and I was like, 'Now I'm gonna kill you cause you not only taking from me, you taking from my kids so now you got to die.'

Crazy Jay stopped only after learning the whereabouts of his car, which, minus its radio, was parked nearby. He then picked up a large bowl and smashed the TV, thereby ensuring that the robber would have to check out of the motel that day. Able to recoup $200 and his car, Crazy Jay never recovered his son's ring. This clearly incensed him, particularly since he had given the robber special treatment as a drug customer (that is, delivery sales, credit). "You bite the hand that feeds you, ... you need to be disciplined," Crazy Jay explained. Deterrence also was on his mind. "[I]f you ever, ever, ever, decide to do that shit again," he described his thinking, "[remember] this first, cause it gonna be even more severe [next time]."

Mad Dog was sitting in his car with a date when a neighborhood rival approached him menacingly with a gun, forcing him to speed off and lose face in front of his girlfriend. He let two days pass before returning to even the score. "Just to let it cool down some," he explained. "So they [the assailant and his associates] wouldn't be paranoid or nothing. Tripping off who coming down the street [to get them that night]." Mad Dog secured a .45 revolver and car from a local drug user. He chose not to drive his own vehicle for fear it would be recognized as he approached, permitting his intended targets to flee or mount a preemptive strike. Mad Dog picks up the story:

> I pulled around the corner. I saw them out standing next to the car, so I pulled up like it wasn't no problem, like I was just driving through. Pulled up, stopped next to them, went on and looked out of the car. He [the assailant] saw my face. [He] started to turn like he was going by to get something, like he was about to run or

something, [then I] pulled the gun up. I started shooting ... I was
just shooting. I wasn't even aiming ... because the way they was
standing there I figured there ain't no way I could miss ... I shot
about six times.

The cases of Sugar, Crazy Jay, and Mad Dog suggest a critical lack
of coercive power at the moment of the initial affront, making
reflexive retaliation inappropriate. Grievants want respect, but not
at the cost of being seriously injured or killed, and they generally
will submit when placed in a position of extreme vulnerability (see
Luckenbill 1981 on the dynamics of compliance generation). This is
not weakness; it is smart and helps you to survive. Black's initial
reflexive strike was, as readers recall, unsatisfactory, requiring him
to strike a second time. Calculation was his preferred mode of
attack. Though any or all of these respondents may have attacked by
surprise to cover the fact that they were afraid, we have no real way
of knowing if this is true. What we *do* know is that what calculated
strikes may lack in celerity, they can more than make up for in
certainty and severity. Perhaps this is what makes calculated
strikes so attractive. Sneaking up on a violator at a time and place
of your own choosing virtually guarantees retaliatory success.
Because the violator is likely to be in a position of reduced defensibility at the time of the attack, resistance is improbable. This may
extend the duration and intensity of punishment, and thereby sal-
vage and maybe even enhance one's reputation as someone not to be
crossed.

## Deferred Retaliation

Delayed face-to-face retaliation where the delay is not desired is
called "deferred retaliation." Delays may be caused by a number of
factors. The initial violation may not involve face-to-face contact.
The violation may involve face-to-face contact, but reflexive action
may be impossible owing to the setting, circumstances, or some
preemptive strategy employed by the violator. The aggrieved party
may not immediately recognize a violation for what it is (for

example, valuables that are "borrowed" with no intention of their being returned are actually being stolen, but the lender does not realize this at the time). The aggrieved party may not know the identity of the person who crossed them and/or be unable to find that person.

Deferred retaliation typically undergoes a period of incubation first. How long the incubation period lasts depends on how long it takes to ascertain the identity and/or whereabouts of the violator, how long it takes to realize that a "loan" actually is a theft, or how long it takes to get the violator into a sufficiently vulnerable position to make retaliation possible. Such matters are situational, so whether and when deferred retaliation occurs cannot be predicted with certainty. Retaliation that keeps getting deferred will persist in a state of incubation. Eventually, it will move either to non-retaliation or to "imperfect retaliation" – retribution exacted against an innocent third party. As Bottcher (2001:925) illustrates, "... even in cases in which victims are not personally responsible for affronts or harm, some crimes can best be understood as 'practices of collective liability' – victims stand in, so to speak, for wrongs" committed by someone else. More on this possibility shortly.

Black engaged in deferred retaliation after someone "stole" his marijuana during a party. Stole is placed in quotation marks here because, according to Black, the "motherfucker [who took it] left money." In Black's mind, this was irrelevant. "My shit wasn't for sale," he explained. "it was just a simple principle. Somebody went in my shit [and they shouldn't have] ... I ain't no bitch ... I ain't no punk." The following day, an associate told Black who had taken the $10 bag of dope, and he severely beat the so-called thief with a metal pipe. "I hit him upside his motherfucking head and split it there and put a big old pussy in his head."

D-boy also was burglarized, though his loss was considerably larger – his tire rims and car stereo, two televisions, and a DVD player. He obtained a description of the burglar from a neighbor, and he matched it to other clues to make a positive identification. D-boy encountered the thief on the street one afternoon, and heated dialogue quickly gave way to violence. The thief struck first, but D-boy got the better of him. "[H]e swung on me first," D-boy recalled, but he missed and "when he missed I hit him one time and dropped him and he held his eye and moved his hand and it looked like his eye could talk." Despite winning this fight, D-boy remained concerned about counter-retaliation, even though he felt his actions were justified. The man lived close by, knew where to find him, and would undoubtedly be embarrassed after waking "up with a fat-assed purple and red and burgundy eye ... revenge, revenge, revenge," D-Boy explained. "That's all that's on his mind."

Three days after someone smashed his car windows, punctured the tires, and dented the bodywork, Biddle ascertained the likely identity of the vandal. It appeared to be the boyfriend of a woman Biddle was having sex with, behind the man's back. Retaliation did not follow immediately. Biddle needed additional time to piece together information to confirm the vandal's identity. When reprisal finally came, it came opportunistically:

> I popped over [to the woman's house one day]. He [the vandal] was on the front [porch] ... [I] rolled past [and parked in the back] ... get my bat out the trunk ... his [the bat's] name Johnny, [and I came through the house to the front porch] ... and I'm like 'what's up player?' ... He tried to break out and just run cause he knew he was guilty ... I swung the bat. Hit him in the back. He fell. Boom ... [Then I] broke two of his legs ... neighbors came out ... [and] grabbed me [and stopped the beating].

Deferred retaliation also emerged opportunistically for Big Mac and Smoke Dog. Shot twice in the right side with a .22 rifle by his girlfriend's ex-boyfriend, Big Mac spotted the assailant leaving a grocery store some nine months later, "on the humbug" as he put it. "Damn, this look like this dude [that shot me], hear me," he recalled saying to friends he was riding with at the time. "Whip a U-turn around. We pull up. It's him. So he didn't notice that it was like actually me until we got to hopping out of the car and it was like too late [for him to react] ... jumped on him real bad ... whooped on him ... stomped him in the ground." The violator apparently was lucky to get off as easily as he did. "If I would've had a gun," Big

Mac revealed, "I probably would have shot him ... I ain't gonna lie about that." Smoke Dog's antagonist, meanwhile, actually approached *him*, unaware that he was out for revenge. This individual had slapped Smoke Dog's mother during a drug transaction earlier that morning, not knowing that they were related. In a strange twist of fate, the violator approached Smoke Dog later that afternoon to buy $20 worth of heroin. Shooting dice with a friend at the time, Smoke Dog momentarily left under the pretext of retrieving the requested heroin from his stash spot. He returned with a 9 millimeter instead:

> We shootin dice and shit ... gambling like a motherfucker. Motherfucker [the violator] hit me in the shoulder [tap, tap, tap, tap]. 'Damn man, what's up?' 'What's up with you?' ... Let me get two of them pills ... Stay right here. I'm gonna go get that for you. I had my car in the back. I had a 9 millimeter too. One of them little bitty 9 millimeters, about that big [motioning] ... it was a proper little nine, too, Eighteen shots, this little though you hear me [motioning] ... [I went back to him and he] gave me $20. [I put the money in my pocket and acted like I was going to give him the heroin but I pulled my gun out instead.] Boom! ... - creased him [with the bullet]. 'Damn, what you doin?' [he said]. 'Yeah I know you hit my mama, that's what I'm doin'. He tried to run on me. I hit [shot] him in the ass. Boom ... he ran around this car [parked on the street] ... every time I try to run around the car, he runnin around the car, like ... little kids' shit, cat and mouse shit ... man, it's broad daylight, Bruce, it's broad daylight. Old people outside. Little kids outside. Girls out there playing double-dutch, jump rope. I'm straight shooting at this man - ... dumping [bullets] in broad daylight ... [Then] I got to hearing those sirens and I ran.

Big D and Jay were beneficiaries of no such serendipity. Big D was forced to recuperate for several weeks after being stabbed in a drug dispute – once right above the heart, leaving a four-inch scar and a second time across her neck, just below the throat, leaving a six-inch-long Colombian necktie-style wound. Two weeks after leaving the hospital, Big D caught up with the violator – coincidentally, at the same location where the slashing occurred. She approached the woman with a .45 caliber handgun and "blew her motherfucking brains out," as she recalled. The woman survived, but in a comatose-like state. "She just a vegetable," Big D said matter-of-factly. "She might as well be [dead.]" Likewise, Jay had to wait somewhere between two and three months before retaliating against his "bitch ass" aunt, who had stolen $350 from a cookie jar in his home. "[S]he seen me put my money up there [after a drug sale]," Jay explained, "when I left [the house, she came back and took it]." Jay claimed he "wasn't that hot at first," but after it became clear that his aunt was "dodging" him, he decided to visit his grandmother, knowing the aunt would "pop up sooner or later." Eventually she did and Jay "caught that bitch just the way I wanted to," grabbing her by the back of her head and punching and kicking her. Though the aunt subsequently called the police, leading to Jay's arrest, he reportedly felt a sense of "relief like the money [she] stole was [used to] wipe [her] ass with."

## Sneaky Retaliation

Delayed retaliation where the delay is desired by the avenging party, but where revenge is exacted without face-to-face contact with the violator is called "sneaky retaliation." Because the delay is desired, this implies a certain amount of strategizing on the part of the grievant. That is, the grievant wants to "get" the violator in a particular way, and this requires a period of planning and pre-paration. Because such strikes do not involve face-to-face contact, it appears that grievants want to keep their identities secret – to mini-mize the risk of detection and arrest and/or of counter-retaliation. But there may be more to it than this, especially where the insti-gating affront did not involve face-to-face contact. When that is the case, the wronged party may use sneaky retaliation as a way of matching their response to the initial violation, thereby taking a proverbial "eye for an eye."

Consider the case of Block, a street-level drug dealer who hid $600 worth of crack in a vacant building for safekeeping.

Apparently someone saw him do this, and seized the stash after he left. Returning to find his drugs missing, Block was "fucking mad" but remained unaware of who stole the cache for about a month. Discovery came when the thief revealed the heist to his girlfriend who, unknown to him, was friends with Block's girlfriend. A subsequent phone conversation between Block and his girlfriend exposed the violator:

> [H]e told his gal and his gal cool with my gal ... [but] he didn't know they was cool ... they just gossiping on the phone ... he was bragging to his gal about it and she running her mouth ... and [then it got back to me].

Waiting an additional two weeks, Block enlisted a friend to set up a drug deal to lure the thief out of his house. Block and a third associate then burglarized the dwelling, netting two ounces of powder cocaine, an ounce of crack, a drug scale, and over $300 in cash – considerably more than had been lost during the instigating theft. Asked why he chose burglary as opposed to violent reprisal, Block responded that he was "playing his [the violator's] game ... I'm playing him the same way [he played me]."

In a subsequent interview with one of Block's accomplices, it emerged that the burglary had turned into a robbery. The co-offender reported that he and Block had waited for the thief to return home, and attacked him as he walked into the house. Block, however, did not take part in the robbery directly; the co-offender said he did all the talking, threatening, and beating. Both men, however, were masked, preserving the offense's sneaky nature: There was contact, but it was not, strictly speaking, "face-to-face."

Clearly, it pleased Block that the violator could not ascertain who victimized him. Knowing that you've been exploited, but not knowing who did it, can be agonizing. No amount of searching will turn up the needed information so long as the perpetrators keep their mouths shut. Frustration may not subside significantly for some time, and Block's strategy was intended to make the violator's blood boil. Subsequent interaction with the antagonist has convinced him that his strategy is working:

| Block: | [W]e see him every day ... He's pissed ... he riding around mad. |
|---|---|
| Jacobs: | Do you think he knows that you did it? |
| Block: | If he does he might have an idea because he knows he got me. He probably like, 'That nigger Block probably got me.' But I'm watching him though. See what I'm saying? I'm watching him. |

Similarly, Teaser rejoiced after breaking into the home of the man that had "played" her for sex with no intention of entering into a committed relationship, giving her gonorrhea in the process. Besides stealing $2,000 cash, jewelry, and a TV, she also slashed his tires, which were outfitted with expensive Spreewell custom wheels; the rims were not damaged, but the violator would have to order new ones to fit the new tires he had to purchase for his vehicle. "[H]e's stressed up," she remarked with obvious satisfaction, "and ... don't look the same, don't dress the same, he's like he lost out because he don't have any money ... [I feel good about that] cause he shouldn't have done me that way." This non-violent incident stands in stark contrast to one in which Teaser beat a man with a baseball bat after he slapped and spit on her in a nightclub. This incident was public, the STD was not, and Teaser desired symmetry of method. "It's a difference when you embarrass somebody and when you don't," she explained. "Didn't too many people know what happened between me and the [guy who gave me the STD]. But this [nightclub assault] was in front of everybody ... this guy embarrassed me in front of people." Female on male direct retaliatory violence is particularly rare, for reasons specified in the next chapter, but gender's role in mediating retaliatory decisions is separate and distinct from the timing and contact issues explored here.

The fact that a strike is sneaky does not preclude it from involving excessive violence. Indeed, a sneaky approach may allow the wronged party to use more force than a more reflexive (or public) response would permit. Red, for instance, accidentally spilled a glass of cognac on a man at a local tavern. The man responded by "knock[ing] the shit" out of Red, without giving him an opportunity to apologize first. Other patrons inside the bar witnessed the assault, including the man's date, a woman Red vaguely knew. Embarrassed and enraged, Red left the bar and went to his vehicle, where he retrieved his pistol and sat waiting for four hours. When the man finally left the tavern – drunk – Red attacked, maximizing the shock value by sneaking up and shooting him numerous times from behind. Although Red could have responded to the affront more publicly and immediately, this would have prevented him from employing the level of coercive force he felt was justified by the circumstances. Attacking by surprise also reduced the chances that somebody would witness the strike. The rage Red felt that night was still palpable during our interview with him, which took place months after the incident:

> [A] man don't never put his hand on another man ... ain't never in my life had a motherfucker smack me before. Beside my mom and my dad. Them are the only ones I ever had in my life smack me ... I'm forty-three years old ... I'm stone cold, that's the bottom line, the dude should never had put his hands on me. He should have never smacked me ... [I was] straight up angry.

V-O, Smoke Dog, and Paris opted to use proxies to do the retributive work for them, though their reasons for doing so varied. Exposure-minimization was the principal objective for V-O. Encountering a man on the street who had assaulted his cousin in jail, V-O stalled him until an armed associate could drive over "because he'd [the target would] know us." Smoke Dog reported being at a point in his life where discretion was starting to seem like the better part of valor. After someone slapped his sister, he enlisted his "little homies" to exact vengeance on his behalf. "I'm trying to be a G [a wise street criminal] about it now," he explained. "[I]f it's too hard for me and I can't handle it then I go hire my little homies ... they just love to shoot." Paris's reasons for relying on retaliatory proxies were more immediately pragmatic: The police happened upon him right after he was beaten, robbed, and carjacked. Thus he would be an obvious suspect in any crime of violence committed against his attackers:

> Why didn't I do it? Cause I didn't want to take the blame. Cause the police already had my name or whatever, you know cause they picked me up from the ambulance or what ever and I know they just gonna be like, 'Maybe this guy did it" or whatever.

Retaliation by proxy is sneaky because the violator is unable to link the strike directly to the wronged party. Though grievants could instruct the proxy to let the violator know they are behind the strike, this seldom seems to happen.[3] Grievants with sufficiently fierce street reputations need not worry about looking like "punks" by having someone else do their dirty work for them. What matters, at least for some respondents, is retribution, not who carries it out. "As long as it's taken care of," Moon illustrates, "it don't matter [if I do it or I have somebody do it for me]." Of course, not all offenders who are victimized can make this claim, especially where, for example, an affront is serious and/or hits particularly close to home. Such circumstances typically call for self-help in the literal sense of the term.

## Imperfect Retaliation

Delayed retaliation without face-to-face contact where the delay is not desired is called "imperfect retaliation." Imperfect retaliation occurs when grievants exact vengeance from someone other than the person who wronged them. Typically, it is an option of last resort, adopted only after grievants have tried and failed to identify, locate, and/or punish the actual wrongdoer. Imperfect retaliation typically accomplishes one or more of three goals: message-sending, loss recovery, and anger release.

Kimmy, a female stripper, lost $900 to a fellow dancer during a private motel sex party. Kimmy had gone into the bathroom to have sex with one of the partygoers, and asked another stripper to watch

---

[3] There were no mentions of it in the transcripts though, in all candor, we did not specifically ask respondents whether they gave such instructions.

her purse. Her co-worker agreed, but ended up stealing the money in Kimmy's absence. Kimmy had still not managed to track down the thief at the time we interviewed her. But a week after the theft, Kimmy's cousin had spotted a car belonging to one of the thief's friends in the parking lot of a local 7-Eleven store. The cousin telephoned Kimmy, who jumped into her badly damaged car and rammed it into the parked vehicle. She then grabbed a metal pole from her car, ran into the store, and attacked the woman. In the following passage, Kimmy explains why she did what she did, why it was better to strike imperfectly than not at all, and why she failed to obtain closure via this imperfect strike:

> [I] beat her partner's ass ... fuck her cause that's her [the violator's] friend and she knows some shit about [the stolen money] ... When she seen my face she know what the hell I'm up there for ... [But I want the violator to] see [by beating her friend] that I'm not playing ... even if it stops right there I know I did something ... that's the closest thing I could [do] ... [But] I'm gonna kill this bitch [the violator] ... Anybody fuck with my money ... [is] fucking with my daughter cause that's where my money go ... Even if I get my $900 back I'm gonna beat her ass anyway ... I could be ... on my deathbed. I swear I get my ass up and try to beat this bitch's ass. I swear I will.

Goldie adopted a similar strategy after failing to locate any of the four individuals who robbed him at a bus stop of a gold necklace. Three months after the robbery, Goldie spoke to a man who claimed to know the whereabouts of at least one of the robbers. He directed Goldie to a neighborhood just four blocks away. Goldie went there, and he spotted the robber's younger brother. Goldie picks up the story:

> I saw his little brother and I went up to him, I didn't have my burner [gun] on me at the time so I'm just like, 'Where's your brother at?' 'I don't know where he is, I don't know where he is.' I'm like, 'Well tell him Goldie, he's gonna holler at him about something.' Instantly he already knew, I could see that in his face,

that he already knew. 'So you're Goldie? OK well I'll tell him, I'll tell him.' I'm like, are you shocked or whatever. So I come back. His brother's still in the same damn spot, but this time I got a burner with me. I'm looking for trouble, cause I know he's somewhere around here, cause his little brother's still around, you know what I'm saying? Saw his little brother again, I'm like, 'Where's your brother, I still ain't seen your brother.' 'No I still ain't seen him, still ain't seen him,' and at the same time I'm seeing him rumbling with a little pack that he had, I guess it was some crack or whatever. So I'm like, 'Well you just give me that right there, that'll pay for it.' 'What do you mean give you that?' 'You just give me that right there.' So I show him a little burner [gun], like, and he's like, 'OK, I ain't doing anything, he did it.' So now he's telling on his brother. 'So where is he?' ... 'Oh I can't tell you where. So I'm like, 'Well you can take for it then.' [I got] about $400 [cash], $1300 of dope ... [told] him to go back and tell his brother, and as he was walking off he was kind of mumbling something, you know what I'm saying? So I smacked him in the back of the head with the strap, you know what I'm saying? He fall to the ground, get up running and I'm shouting, 'Tell you brother I'm looking for him.'

Imperfect reprisal is best considered an interim measure rather than a replacement for direct retribution. Generally speaking, there is no substitute for symmetrical vengeance. The individual who actually commits the violation must ultimately be punished. No one should believe that they have escaped retribution, lest they inspired to commit another transgression. It may be true, however, that some imperfect strikes are "less imperfect" than others. As Kimmy and Goldie imply, the closer the imperfect target is to the actual violator, the less "psychological distance" there is from the goal of direct retaliation (see Miller et al. 2003:91). Strikes committed against someone "close" to the violator may also help to flush him or her out, which makes direct reprisal easier to accomplish. If material losses are recovered as part of the retaliatory attack, the original violation may lose some of its original sting. And few indirect measures are better at communicating the message that grievants are mad, looking, poised to attack, and nearby than attacks of the sort launched by Kimmy and Goldie. Chapter Five explores the issues relevant to displaced vengeance in full detail.

## Non-retaliation

Despite the unforgiving logic of the retaliatory ethic, not every disagreement culminates in conflict and not every conflict results in serious violence (see Luckenbill and Doyle 1989:425; Baron, Forde, and Kennedy 2001). Non-retaliation sometimes occurs by default: The violator may never be identified, located, or encountered in a setting conducive to reprisal. But grievants sometimes make a conscious decision not to retaliate. And no matter what really motivates that decision, they must justify their inaction as something other than cowardice because, on the street, failure to act is almost automatically interpreted as weakness.

Grievants who choose not to retaliate may stake one of two claims to deflect imputations of cowardice. The first involves a semantic sleight of hand in which grievants position themselves "above" the wrongdoing, suggesting that it was not serious enough to worry about. By downplaying the violation, grievants affirm their superiority even as they submit to what is otherwise a status-reducing action. After losing several hundred dollars in a drug deal gone bad, Gerry thus told us that payback was not "worth the time" – implying that the loss was chump change for a person of his status. "[N]o, it's got to be some money [involved before it's worth retaliating]," he insisted. For E, the nature of the loss was less salient than the person who caused it, though status remained equally relevant to his assessment of the perceived harm; a homeless man whose obvious desperation had driven him to theft made retaliation moot. "People like that gonna kill themselves," he mused. "Homeless guy don't mean it; there ain't no point in hurting him." For Player, non-seriousness was a function of time, though status remained at least tangentially implicated in his account. The decade that passed from the day he was robbed and pistol-whipped to the day he ran into the violator undermined the salience of reprisal. "It happened so fucking long ago," Player recounted. "I'd almost damn forgotten about it [by the time I saw the responsible party again] ... Sometimes you get robbed and you got to accept it."

The second justification for not retaliating is that a pre-existing relationship between the grievant and the violator negates the need. Serious violence often involves people who have strong ties, but short relational distance can also play a powerful role in encouraging victims to "turn the other cheek." Hops, for example, was shot by a close friend, and despite nearly being killed, elected not to pursue the matter. He and the assailant had grown up next door to each other, currently worked in the same neighborhood, and lunched together on a frequent basis. In other words, the bond between the two men was sufficiently strong for Hops to recognize his own culpability in the event, creating the empathy necessary to preempt a retaliatory strike:

> It was a guy that I like grew up with and we really stayed like next door to each other and both us worked in the community ... Well we didn't actually work together but we met up at lunch times and we were just jesting around, joking around and stuff we do every day at work, and we were just so used to talking about each other and making fun of each other ... And one day the guy ... I don't know what he had on his mind, he must have had something on his mind the whole time, the whole day. We meet up at lunch and we usually jesting and joking. I play with him and he's like, he don't wanna play ... So he was like, 'Man, fuck you, I ain't playing today.' I'm like, 'Don't give me that.' The guy straight turned around, pulls out a gun, and said, 'Motherfucker, I ain't playing today.' Got up in his face, and I'm like, 'Fuck you with your gun.' ... [H]e shot me in my head and I ducked, so he got the weapon and we tussled. I'm trying to get the gun and it went off again and he shot me in the stomach and my hand ... took [me] to the hospital ... after a week and a half I got out. And I really started to look at things different. I started looking at my life. I could have been gone just like that ... The reason I didn't go after him was because we were friends and then I really looked at the situation. It was my fault because the guy did say he didn't feel like it today and I tussled around with him and ended up being shot ... Yeah, ended up being shot. Man we just came back

friends, let bygones be bygones. As time went on, as I got well, I never looked back.

The protective effect of strong ties may even be extended to strangers in cases where a violator is affiliated with one of the grievant's friends. Jay Moon, for instance, pardoned someone who defrauded him of $1,000 because he knew the violator's mother. "I just took it as a loss," he recalled. "His mama is like my mama. My mama is like his mama … I don't want to hurt the dude." Likewise, Goldie was unsuccessfully carjacked by the cousin of a friend. Despite desperately wanting to retaliate, he decided not to strike back because he was so "tight" with the friend that he "couldn't even look in my boy's eye [if I did]." Goldie went on to explain that he and his friend had "done dirt [serious crime] together, they had "done got fucked up together [and] fucked hos [women] together. I mean, like, just done too much stuff together for me to fuck up his little cousin."[4] Struck in the head with a baseball bat by the sister of his girlfriend, TC also opted not to retaliate. The wound required twenty two staples to close, impaired TC's memory for months, and nearly killed him, but the woman was so-called family. Even more relevant – at least in this instance – was the fact that TC's brother recently had been executed, inspiring TC to think about the impact his own death would have on his mother. "Yeah, he [my brother] got that [legal injection] … so you know, to show my mama how much I love her [I didn't retaliate], so I wouldn't end up like him."

Short relational distance not only may decrease the probability of retaliation, it also may reduce its severity. The distinction is important inasmuch as it suggests that relational ties can mediate reprisal's form, and not merely its occurrence. Pooh Bear thus retaliated against a man she considered to be "family" for stealing $7,000 worth of crack from her, but not with the severity she would have used on a stranger. She had several male friends beat up the violator, knocking out his teeth in

---

[4] Goldie's decision was perhaps easier because the violator reportedly did not know it was Goldie he tried to carjack until well after the attempted offense. But even if this information were known, our sense was that the perpetrator's connection would still have lessened Goldie's wrath.

an unsuccessful bid to get the drugs back. For Pooh Bear, letting the thief live is tantamount to "letting [the violation] ride." That "dude should have been six feet under," she insisted. The bottom line is that, in the violent world of retaliatory street justice, a claim of relational closeness may serve as a powerful face-saving mechanism where grievants choose, for whatever reason, not to retaliate or to inflict reduced punishment on the violator; it permits them to move beyond the affront without being stigmatized as a coward by their peers.

## The Retaliatory Calculus in Action

This chapter has outlined a typology of criminal retaliation organized around two axial factors: whether or not reprisal occurs immediately after the affront, and whether or not it involves face-to-face contact with the violator. Non-retaliation is also explored. The various branches of this model and its assorted pathways are depicted schematically in Figure 3.1.

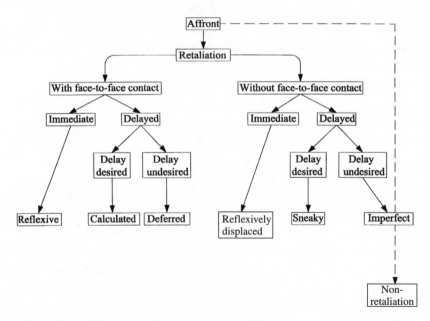

Figure 3.1 Schematic showing assorted branches and pathways in criminal retaliation.

The reports from the offenders we talked to clearly underscore the importance of direct confrontation in retaliatory strikes. Retaliation without face-to-face contact with the violator – be it sneaky or imperfect – may deliver harm, but not the kind of harm that most offenders believe cuts to the core of street values. An essential part of payback involves letting violators know that the person they wronged has evened the score. Otherwise, violators may be left with the impression that the victim is "soft" and therefore has accepted the affront.

The fact that counter-strikes often exceed violations in both intensity and magnitude reaffirms the notion that security, and not just the pursuit of justice, is driving the retaliatory process. Obviously, some violations are worse than others, and this is important because the degree of moralistic outrage reserved for a violation derives largely from the level of disrespect inferred by it (Miller 2001). Our interviews suggest that violators who sneak up on you from behind, who gang up on you, who take something from you when you are not around (thereby trying to conceal their identity), or who initiate a violation without following through merit especially punitive attention. Such affronts are perceived as "cowardly." They suggest a violator who either is trying to avoid the consequences of their actions or who is wronging someone in a way not sanctioned by the code of the street.

In street culture, how violators commit an affront says a lot about their character. Violators perceived to be "shady" make grievants want to track them down that much more, and punish them with greater fury: "How dare you do that to me or do it in the way you did it. Now you're really going to pay." Failing to retaliate against affronts like these makes grievants look as cowardly as the initiating violation was shameless. Non-action legitimates the affront and compounds the humiliation associated with it (Fitness 2001). And that humiliation is likely to be especially strong where grievants "personalize" the attack – that is, when they believe they were singled out for the violation rather than being chosen at random (see Jones and Davis 1965 on personalism inferences; also see DeRidder et al. 1999). In street culture, attacks are often perceived to be personal forms of condemnation.

The primacy of defending security, as opposed to achieving simple justice, is seen even more clearly when strikes are delayed. Delay introduces separation between the "aversive stimulus" (that is, the violation) and reprisal, which should "unbound" rationality and moderate the attack rather than intensify it. Instead, anger seems to boil, not simmer down. Delays give grievants an opportunity to mull over what has happened and to become more incensed rather than less. Shock "gives way to indignation and then outrage" as the magnitude of the violation sinks in (Rather 2001). This "rumination" process, as Bies and Tripp call it, allows grievants to revisit the violation mnemonically, digging up new facts and evidence "overlooked in the initial processing of the violation ... [and] to 'discover' more personalistic causes of the violation," which enhances the transgressor's blame (Bies and Tripp 1996:254). Anger is especially intense if there is mounting frustration about the identity or whereabouts of the violator. The reprisal that follows is intended not only to restore what grievants lost, but also to "compensate" them for the cognitive burden they have shouldered since the affront.[5]

The logical possibilities of retaliation against a backdrop of situational constraints are intriguing, but so are the factors that mediate retributive choices when several options are realistically available. Why, for example, choose sneaky reprisal over calculated reprisal when circumstances permit either or both? Given that timing and contact are the critical orienting dimensions, and that each dimension mediates behavior (at least in a volitional sense) only when delay is desired, risk sensitivity would appear to be the relevant explanation. This is obvious, and also somewhat tautological. Any tactic that reduces a grievant's chances of encountering resistance, counter-retaliation, or arrest betrays sensitivity to risk; delays and striking without contact minimize all of these potential

---

[5] This is probably true only for a finite period as a result of the basic psychophysiological processes of anger. But this period may be longer in street culture (than in comparable settings) where law is unavailable because of the importance and fragility of respect.

hazards. More instructive, perhaps, are the factors that condition risk sensitivity by discouraging the desire for face-to-face contact and encouraging a preference for delay. Vertical distances between disputants (Black 1983) and the presence or absence of third parties (Cooney 1998) merit special consideration here.

The individuals who wronged the offenders we interviewed were strangers, loose acquaintances, friends, and in at least one instance, family members, of varying, though roughly equivalent, statuses, and the preference for direct contact was fairly uniform. As status differences become more pronounced, this picture may change – a pattern that appears to hold for both upward and downward revenge. Thus, low-status parties who retaliate against those of markedly higher status may face severe consequences, and, knowing this, they may elect not to do so (see, for example, Homans 1961; Kim et al. 1998). In such cases, reprisal often is better performed sneakily, or redirected against parties perceived to be less formidable and/or having little or nothing to do with the violation in question. Though it is conceivable for low-status grievants to want bold, face-to-face strikes as a way of enhancing their reputations, the likely costs will often be perceived as sufficiently high to deter such action. High-status grievants appear to prefer face-to-face strikes against lower-status violators for precisely the opposite reason – striking without contact permits someone of lower status to seize your respect, which brings you down to that person's level and fully announces to others that you can be victimized with impunity. Sometimes, however, the status imbalance is so great that direct reprisal ceases to be meaningful or necessary. For grievants like Smoke Dog, for example, such violations are treated as "petty" and "not worth the time."

Third parties are relevant for issues of timing. Provided that their presence does not generate coercive power imbalances for either disputant, or introduce levels of natural surveillance sufficient to deter the behavior contemplated, the presence of audiences generally increase the importance of celerity. Reputations are "on the line" when violations are committed against someone in public, but this is especially true when others are around to witness them directly. The

71

dilemma for many grievants is that situational circumstances often do not permit the level of punishment they desire to inflict at the moment a violation occurs. Trading celerity for severity is difficult, but logical when the "content" of the lesson is more important than the rapidity with which it is delivered.[6]

Waiting, at least in part, is a function of deterrence objectives, but if a desire to avoid the potential consequences of acting quickly invariably trumped the urge for payback, retaliation would almost always be delayed. It also would rarely involve face-to-face contact or be unduly excessive. Excess is especially noteworthy irrespective of timing, or even contact, because disproportionate strikes, as affronts in themselves, tend to inspire counter-grievances, and then reprisal, as a way of restoring reciprocity (see Tedeschi and Felson 1994:245). As touched on in Chapter Two, the street-criminal underworld is one of the few settings in which strong bilateral retaliatory capacities result in mutual escalation rather than mutual deterrence (see Ohbuchi and Saito 1986 on power imbalance in aggression). Though defiance, as opposed to deterrence, in the face of punishment is by no means unique to street offenders (Blau 1964; Homans 1961; Molm 1994; Sherman 1993), the sensitivity to violations makes it especially likely in this context. Lacking traditional sources of respect – their occupational and familial roles cannibalized by

---

[6] We recognize the obvious benefits of identifying particular contextual circumstances that "produce" one type of retaliatory response over another (given the possible occurrence of multiple types), but the data did not seem to permit it. After analyzing the nature of the violation (violent/non-violent), the context in which it occurred (public/private), the apparent risk of sanction threats at the time the violation occurred (both formal and informal), apparent status differences between grievants and violators at the time of the offense, and apparent relational distances between grievants and violators ("apparent" because it had to be intuited from the transcripts), we could discern no particular reason or reasons why one modality emerged over another – with a single exception, and possibly one more: Reflexive strikes, relative to the other types, seemed to involve less physically threatening violations and an opportunity to strike spontaneously, while sneaky strikes often seemed to involve affronts without contact and violators who were known to the grievant at the time of the affront or shortly thereafter. We initially thought that deferred strikes involved violations without contact, and that calculated strikes required grievants to have a deficit of coercive power when the violation occurred, but these criteria were not necessarily distinguishing. Variation seemed to be more a function of choice in context than context by itself.

persistent poverty and high rates of family disruption (Anderson 1999; Rosenfeld, Jacobs, and Wright 2003; Wilson 1996) – street offenders' reputations depend almost exclusively on how they display and handle themselves in interaction. Disadvantage and marginalization, moreover, reduce the threshold at which any given action is considered to be offensive, resulting in paranoid attributions of hostile intent (see, for example, Dodge et al. 1990). Because such hostility derives ultimately from structural sources over which individuals have little control, excessive responses emerge as compensation and catharsis (on violence as catharsis, see Tedeschi and Felson 1994). This explains why a "relatively small effort targeted at the appropriate point can produce [a] disproportionate effect ...." (Gabriel 1998:1341).

It may be true, however, that different retaliatory modalities have distinct deterrent capacities net of punishment severity. Though strikes involving face-to-face contact (reflexive, calculated, and deferred) have the highest potential for specific deterrence – the lesson is directed at the party responsible for the wrong – they also carry the greatest risk of triggering defiance. Strikes that lack face-to-face contact reduce the risk of defiance, assuming violators remain unaware of the motive and source of the strike, but sacrifice specific deterrence in the process. Sneaky retaliation seems especially vulnerable to this problem: Strikes performed by someone other than the person wronged, or initiated long after the instigating violation, may signal weakness, especially if the violator never realizes that the harm inflicted was retaliatory in nature (as will often be the case with sneaky attacks). Sneaky strikes may succeed in exacting payback, but if the reason for the strike and the identity of the attacker remain unknown, they may appear to be random acts of anti-social behavior – leaving violators undeterred from committing subsequent affronts, and perhaps even more motivated to do so because now they too have lost something. And general deterrence, obviously, is not possible unless grievants brag about getting even, which undermines the very reason for sneaky revenge.

The wide range of retaliatory options available to offenders who have been wronged suggests that their rationality may be less bounded than often is believed. Whereas street criminals typically weigh only a small amount of the information theoretically available to them (Johnson and Payne 1986:173), our findings indicate that more contemplative strategies may be employed when it comes to retaliation. Such procedures need not be lengthy or extensive. Time pressure, threat, and uncertainty have a powerful tendency to increase focus, resulting in sharper analytic clarity and more efficient decision-making (see, for example, Arkes and Ayton 1999; Khatri and Ng 2000). Situational constraints may advance this process. Thus, bounding rationality may actually force the number of choices to expand in the offending moment. The need for reciprocity is too important *not* to consider multiple options, and reprisal might otherwise be insufficiently retributive or pedagogical if performed without adequate attention to contextual cues. This seeming expansion is striking only insofar as it occurs against a backdrop of intense anger, and rational choice itself is thought to break down in anger's presence (Exum 2002). But anger, when inspired by moralistic concerns, may permit alternative retaliatory scripts to emerge, scripts fueled by a hedonistic calculus that is less restrictive and more attuned to communicating the desired punitive message.

# FOUR

# Gender and Retaliation

No factor mediates retributive decision-making more powerfully than gender. Street criminals respond to disputes as *men* and *women* and not simply as offenders. Men obviously dominate the street criminal underworld, and numerous researchers have drawn on the notion of *doing* masculinity – the process whereby men frame their actions to fulfill existing gender roles – to explain their behavior (see, for example, Hamm 2001).

Women represent a far smaller proportion of both the offender and victim population, but females deeply embedded in street-based social networks face the same identity, respect, and security concerns as men. Indeed, maintaining a street persona as someone not to be crossed may be even more critical for female street offenders than for their male counterparts because of the devalued status of femininity in this context. Given prevailing attitudes about women on the streets, especially those linked to passivity and physical weakness, females must negotiate unique challenges if they are to use retaliatory tactics successfully. "Doing masculinity" is not an acceptable explanation for female retribution – whether it occurs against men or other women – nor does it seem appropriate to characterize male on female reprisal in this overly broad way, especially given patriarchal proscriptions against harming women.

Because existing norms sometimes define women as inappropriate targets of serious street violence, this may encourage some *males* to adopt non-violent tactics to retaliate against them. Inter-gender aggression is framed within a number of contradictory contingency norms, and further nuanced with flexible definitions of aggression itself (Miller and White 2003). Unpacking these issues is the principal goal of this chapter. The best way to do this is to offer a typology broken down by sex of the primary disputants.

## Male-on-Male Retaliation

For male street criminals, determined reactions to perceived affronts are essential not only for maintaining ontological security but also for reaffirming their status *as men*. Such reactions become especially important when violations call into question an offender's masculinity. On some level, all violations do this, but certain violations challenge masculinity more directly and vividly than others, and such violations dramatically highlight the ways in which gender influences retaliation.

In a contextual sense, there was no source more likely to promote masculinity challenges than the nightclub scene. Nightclubs and bars are social venues in which men strive to establish reputations and accumulate masculine capital in front of others (Oliver 1994). While the role played by alcohol in the etiology of club disputes cannot be discounted, the scene is by definition a cinematic one: People go there to see and to be seen, which puts a premium on performance that is in turn amplified by the ubiquitous presence of bystanders. Such conditions intensify the perceived gravity of a given slight and enhance the likely severity of the requisite social control response.

Red, for example, accidentally bumped into another man at a bar, for which the man "bitch slapped" Red. "[I] spilled my drink on him," Red recalled, "he just got up and knocked the shit out of me ... [he] smacked me [with an] open hand ... Everyone was watching so ... it made me look bad." Red went out to the parking lot, where he waited and then shot the violator several times – a response that demonstrates not only how a minor incident (an accidental bump in a bar) can escalate into something that ends lethally, but also the way in which the public nature of an affront to manhood fuels vicious payback: The fact that Red was wronged as a *man* was more salient than the fact that he was wronged as an *offender*. The open-handed "bitch slap" publicly undermined his masculinity, triggering a response that, even by the unforgiving logic of the street code, was strikingly asymmetrical.

Most of the disputes between club-hopping males involved competition for a woman, though few of our respondents claimed to have initiated these conflicts. In those rare situations in which interviewees said that they *did* start the fight, the violence is framed not as a response to losing the woman, but rather as a reaction to the patronizing attitude displayed by the other male during the inter-action. Icy Mike's description is typical:

> We was at the club. Motherfucker was trying to haul out with one of my little bitches. I don't give a fuck about the bitch cause I got somebody at home. It don't even matter, but the thing is this old boy is trying to holler at the bitch and then he want to try and throw it in my face like, 'I'm on this bitch, what you gonna do about it?' ... I don't give a fuck about her, you can fuck her. But he's getting too high with this shit, he's feeling too confident with himself ... so I got to let him know, 'You tripping, you showing your ass up to this motherfucking doll' ... I tried to keep it all peaceful and shit, but he want to take it all the wrong way.

Icy Mike made it explicit that he had no attachment to, or invest-ment in, the woman in question. It is the perceived disrespect dis-played by the other man toward him that triggered his resort to violence.

A majority of the men who became embroiled in violent alter-cations over females reported being on the other side of such exchanges, which, in practice, meant that they had been challenged because they were hitting on or disrespecting someone else's woman. Recall the man from Chapter Three who vandalized Biddle's car after discovering that Biddle was having sex with his girlfriend. Speezy's case also is exemplary. Confronted in a skating rink by "some guy telling me about talking to his lady," Speezy told the man "it wasn't like that," but the man persisted. "Next thing I know," Speezy recalled, "he's pushing me, got on like that and I got off the skating arena, then came back and asked him what was up ... He came out, he was like, whatever, so we had to fight ... We got to fighting, fighting on the ground, scrambling this and that . . . Cause his lady friend can talk to me and I can talk to her."

There was a strong propensity for male-on-male disputes to escalate, irrespective of the context or involvement of females. In practice, this meant that the possibility of the use of firearms was never remote. In street culture, a readiness for "gun play" is what sets "real men" apart from pretenders, who talk bad and gesture menacingly but fail to translate talk into action. Red thus encountered the younger brother of a man he recently had shot at a local business; the encounter erupted almost instantaneously into a pitched gun battle that spilled out into the parking lot. "We had a shootout . . . coming out of [a store] . . . I was going in," Red recalled. "He was coming out . . . he had a weapon on him. Fuck it, so we just went at it. Just started shooting at each other . . . I didn't get hit . . . He didn't get hit . . . I was aiming to shoot to kill him . . . I'm saying if I could have really got up on him like I really wanted to, I would have shot his head off . . . [People were] moving out of the way . . . I mean when you shooting . . . you ain't trying to hit on innocent bystanders . . . but when you shoot . . . you ain't got no steering wheel on the bullets."

The aim in such gunfights was not invariably lethal. Cavalier statements about having "put him down" or "he can't come back on me now" notwithstanding, many of the men in our sample reported that they sought only to wound their opponents. The goal, at least in some cases, was to reestablish an aura of dominance over antagonists rather than to eliminate them altogether. "I shot him and I know I shot him," D-Boy illustrates, "I didn't shoot to kill him, but I shot him just to let him know. I put a hot one in your ass." Further reinforcing his non-lethal intent, D-Boy explained that he had shot this same person in the past.

Obviously, not all male-on-male retaliation involved the use of firearms; sometimes, the combatants were unarmed when the conflict began, so cruder weapons like baseball bats or, most commonly, fists and feet would be used instead. The strikes may have been less lethal as a result – bullets kill and seriously injure more readily than do fists – but the physical "beat-down" remains a powerful proclamation of masculine toughness. Chancing upon the man who vandalized his car, Biddle grabbed a Louisville Slugger from his trunk, broke both the man's legs, and said he would have continued the assault had neighbors not restrained him. In a random street corner encounter, Chewy punched the man who falsely claimed that the woman he was "hitting on" was his wife. Chewy not only beat the violator, but "punked" him too – stomping on his hand and striking gratuitous blows to his chest as the man lay prone and vanquished.

The men in our sample disagreed with one another when it came to expressing the masculine logic of *non-contact* strikes, particularly strikes that involved the use of surrogate avengers. Goldie was shot during a street altercation but refused to let his cousin retaliate on his behalf:

| | |
|---|---|
| **Goldie:** | When I got shot my nephew was out there going crazy, calling up saying, "What do you want me to do?" "I want you to do nothing, just calm down, just go on about your life. [The] doctor told me I'd be walking again, gonna still be happy, I'm gonna get them." |
| **Interviewer:** | But why is that, why did you have to do it yourself? |
| **Goldie:** | Cause it was done to me, you know, like it might be somebody do something to my nephew. Most likely he not gonna want me to jump in, he gonna want to do everything on his own. |

As Goldie's comments illustrate, there are important masculinity issues at stake in such cases – the desire to take a personal stand rather than allow others to do your dirty work. But there also are social network considerations at issue; Goldie does not want his nephew to go to jail for something that he sees himself as being responsible for handling. Regardless of the reason, a "stand-up" guy takes care of things himself, which is what Goldie seems to be getting at.

Black likewise disdained the use of retaliatory proxies. "I take care of myself," he told us emphatically. "Why spend the money for it? . . . I got a few little homies out there who would do something.

79

You know, I got some that would do something for free for me, but then I'd have to owe them and I don't want to do that." This example demonstrates that calling on others for assistance may require spending financial or social capital; it incurs debts and obligations and this can run counter to the core demands of street masculinity that lionize independence and autonomy (see, especially, Shover 1996).

As noted in Chapter Three, however, other men framed the use of retaliatory proxies as a sign of their power on the streets, demonstrating that they had a "posse" of subordinates who could handle business for them. When asked if he ever had used others to retaliate for him, E responded: "I've been in a situation like that before. If you can't find them [yourself], then I send my forces out there." Elaborating on a specific incident, he continued: "I had some of my boys beat him [a man he could not find] down and put him in the hospital, break his legs." Asked why he did not participate in the beating, he replied: "I don't like to get my hands dirty. I don't have to get my hands dirty when I got forces. When I got boys who want to do it ... They do it [for free]." Similarly, Icy Mike had no problem relying on the assistance of others by framing the dispute as beneath him: "I didn't want to get my hands dirty, you dig?"

The men in our sample more often mentioned acting as retaliatory proxies for others than they did seeking proxies for themselves. Verbalizations of the role of masculine duty to family members and peers dominated these respondents' explanations of why they were prepared to retaliate on behalf of someone else. Bishop put the matter this way: "I ... always consider if you attack my family, you attack me and if you ask anyone else, especially anyone that grew up in my neighborhood, that's pretty much how the mentality is. You attack the family of somebody, you attack them personally." Red similarly remarked: "It's all about if you hurt somebody that I love, then I'm gonna hurt somebody you love. If you make my mama cry, then I'm gonna make your mama cry, and this gonna go all back and forth." Note the two-way role of family ties in mediating retributive responses. Here, a violation *against* a family member intensifies Bishop's anger. In Chapter Three, recall that familial or quasi-familial ties *to* a violator might preclude retaliation altogether.

Some of the men in our sample described specific incidents in which they had violently victimized other men to punish affronts committed against their female kin. Player, for instance, assaulted a man to get even with him for severely beating his sister. Even afterward, however, Player continued to regard the score as unsettled and, despite the fact that the man was sentenced to prison for assaulting his sister, he still wanted more revenge: "Motherfucker blind[ed] my sister's eye. Broke her fucking nose and just fucked her up... They can't give him enough time. I'm still gonna fuck him up whenever I see him. He's asking for that, man. That's respect. There's no motherfucking way my sister could whoop him, big ol' motherfucker like that. Oh yeah, I'm gonna put a pussy [a gaping wound] in his head whenever I see him... And when I get him to where I know I got him, I'm gonna lay hands on him."

Likewise, Bishop described a lengthy conflict that developed between him and a man who repeatedly had beaten his pregnant sister:

> My sister was seeing this gentleman... [he] knew about me and
> my friends and yet he still insisted on seeing my sister after we
> warned him... I found out that he had got my sister pregnant and
> then refused to take responsibility for it... and then, on top of
> that, he beat her... First we threatened him to try to get him to
> take responsibility, but it didn't work... talked to him, tell him,
> first I was nice to him because he did have some ties in the
> neighborhood... I wanted to keep some peace. When that didn't
> work I got into several confrontations with him and it was getting
> worse each time... [I tried to tell him to] stop touching her, stop
> hitting her... and it started getting worse... a few times he
> walked away with a broken nose, I think we broke his hip one
> time.

The demands of masculinity to protect your kin lie at the core of all of these examples but, significantly, the interviewees also frame the catalyst for their violence as being the failure of their victims to properly enact their masculine roles by assaulting a member of "the weaker sex."

## Male-on-Female Retaliation

The nature of male-on-female retaliation will almost inevitably be complicated by an inherent contradiction in street conceptions of masculinity, whereby men are expected to maintain dominance over women while simultaneously avoiding the use of excessive violence and protecting them from the violent advances of others. Real-world resolution of this contradiction can take several forms. Some men might disregard slights committed against them by women, seeing the perpetrator as so weak and insignificant as not to be worth worrying about. Alternatively, men could enlist female proxies to retaliate for them (sneaky retaliation), or they could adopt physically non-violent methods to exact vengeance. When retaliatory violence occurs outside of domestic relationships, we also might expect men to employ a unique set of rationalizations to explain their behavior, especially because women are widely regarded on the streets as incapable of defending themselves. Keep in mind, however, that the population of concern here is street criminals, whose extra-legal status may well trump chivalry concerns.

Though a few men mentioned using violence against domestic partners, to "keep them in line," most rejected the idea of violently retaliating against women. Duff told us that he "was always raised not to hit a woman, no matter what. I always live by that; my mother was a strong woman so I live by that." V-O echoed these sentiments: "That's just how I was brought up. Taught never to touch a woman." Dub simply said, "I don't hit females." Other men pointed to their perceptions of women's innate weakness as a reason for not using violence against them. As Goldie put it: "I don't go around busting up women or shit like that. Nor pull no gun on them . . . bitch might fuck my car up. So I'd retaliate and fuck her car up . . . It [beating her up] ain't even worth it . . . A man can handle [getting beat up]. Women can't."

On the streets, men tend to define women as helpless and weak; thus they are not seen as representing much of a risk to their safety. Geasy, for example, straightforwardly claimed: "a girl can't hurt you . . . unless you let her." Likewise, Kow reported: "[I] don't get into it [violence] with women. Cause a woman gonna be a woman and she just gonna talk, that what they do, so you can look over a woman quick . . . a woman can't do no harm to you . . . she might just go and get somebody for you, but she won't actually hurt you . . . she a woman, she ain't gonna do nothing to you." And TD concurred, adding that using violence against a woman could undermine his masculinity: "Me, myself, would feel less of a man retaliating on a female, so I [feel] like you have to be equal, so if it was a male it would be a whole different thing."

Despite these strong pronouncements, some of the men in our sample *did* use violence against women, offering up qualifications and exceptions to generally professed norms against such violence to justify their aggression. Kow, for instance, spoke for many of the men in observing that on the streets, when a woman is perceived to be acting like a man, she is likely to be treated as one. The following exchange between Kow and the research team identifies the contradictions in the way in which men on the streetcorner perceive women:

Interviewer:  But a woman can rob you . . . what do you do in that situation?

Kow:  Oh man, you smack the shit out of her. You smack her fucking ass . . . if she man enough to stick her hand in your pocket, you know, it's just like going into your face . . . if you man enough to stick you hand in, you man enough to take the rap.

E offered a very similar explanation when asked if there was a difference between men and woman as targets for retaliatory violence: "[There is] no difference. Why should there be a difference? If she can go out there and do the things a man do, she man enough to get her [payback] like a man." Reinforcing his stance, E described beating up a pregnant woman because she "kept trying to play games with me...playing me against my partners and stuff [so, in response, I] broke her nose, broke her jaw, kicked her all in her stomach and just thumped her down."

TC reported that it was acceptable to use violence against a woman, but only in self-defense: " I don't think [hitting a woman is] OK, but, if it is...defending yourself, then OK...if she came over and hit me, hit me and hit me, then I just fire up and 'pow! pow!' then that's just defending myself...that's totally different." He emphasized that the woman had to pose a real danger, otherwise you should just run away. V-O indicated that before he would resort to violence against a woman she would have to do something "very serious...if she tried to poison me or...setting me up to get hit."

The men in our sample described numerous incidents of male-on-female violence. Most of these incidents involved pugilism rather than weapons, but some still resulted in severe injuries. And although some of the men insisted they would never hit a woman unless she represented a serious threat to their safety, in practice they often retaliated against females for provocations strikingly similar to those that prompted them to take action against other males, for examples, theft, verbal disrespect, or wronging one of their kin.

Occasionally, the men described incidents in which women were treated with no more deference than the males they interacted with on the streets. Player, for example, was trying to track down a man who had not paid him for some drugs when he happened upon one of his female associates. Initially, he claimed to have refrained from harming her, even though he believed that she was covering for her friend: "[I] told her what was up...I didn't hit her. I just made my shit out to her and told her he'd taken my money and don't be so stupid acting like she don't know what's fucking going on." Later in his description of this same encounter, however, the following exchange occurred:

Interviewer: So you beat her, you slapped her around.
Player: Just a little.

Many of the men in our sample discussed male-on-female violence in a similar way: initially denying or downplaying their participation, then admitting to doing it. Smoke Dog is exemplary of this phenomenon:

**Interviewer:** Have you ever retaliated against a woman?
**Smoke Dog:** Only way I'd probably do it is if she try to set me up.

Yet immediately, he begins to elaborate: "I've choked a lot of bitches, pushed they heads against walls and shit...they were playing me man, bitches got to pay." Only one of the male offenders admitted to shooting a woman, and that was in retaliation for a very serious assault during which she slit his throat in an attempt to kill him.

There is another important retaliatory modality in this context: the use of sex as a weapon. For example, some of the male interviewees reported having sex with other women in response to a romantic partner's transgressions against them. TC described using just such a retaliatory tactic:

> With this woman, matter of fact I'm the best thing going for her, I kind of changed her world. But for some reason she feels that...this can't be the cream of the crop, gotta be something better...out there. So what she did, she went out and messed around and found out that...there wasn't anybody better than me, and so what happened was I cheated on her with her cousin, [and made a video tape of the incident]. Take it [the tape] and played it [for her]...[we was] doing extra things I never even done with her. I mean it pissed her off.

Only one man in our sample, V-O, admitted to orchestrating a sexual assault to retaliate against a woman who had wronged him. The female in question had stolen about $300 worth of drugs from him. Two weeks later, he and his male associates found her. V-O explains what happened next: "Everybody got her...well, everybody just all took their turn with her." As noted, this was the only such incident in our data; other offenders vehemently denounced this sort of behavior. E provided a pragmatic reason why he would never use sexual assault to retaliate against a woman who wronged him:

> You use sex, that's rape. I don't go for that, not in my game. She make you mad, smack her around, but don't rape her. You want to kill her, kill her. Take her out, leave her there...killing a woman is better than raping her...cause murder you get a lesser charge. Rape you get a big charge.

The contradictions surrounding the use of violence against women caused some of the men in our sample to enlist the help of female proxies to exact revenge for them. TD provided a clear example of this approach: "[I] always have my girlfriend handle a woman." He then went on to elaborate: "Like my family members are all girls. You know, you got boys that hang together, we got girls that hang together. So if I get involved with a girl, I'd get a girl, the girls would take care of it, and if they have trouble with the boys, then we go help them out." None of these men saw it as cowardly to use a woman as a proxy in such cases. Instead, they portrayed doing so as an appropriate way to circumvent street-based prohibitions against assaulting women.

## Female-on-Female Retaliation

Female-on-female retaliation presents an opportunity to examine Anderson's (1999) contention that the "code of the streets" extends equally to men and women. If Anderson is correct, then the motivation and resolution of retaliatory encounters between women should be broadly similar to those occurring between men (see also Baskin and Sommers 1998). Alternatively, some strains of feminist criminology suggest that female-on-female conflicts should exhibit key differences when compared with those involving male combatants. First, they should be less likely to involve firearms and thus be less lethal. They also should be less likely to involve affronts emanating from public-space activities such as drug dealing, both because women are marginalized from participation in these activities (see Bourgois 1995, 1996; Daly 1989; Maher 1997) and because, compared with men, women are socialized to be more attuned to private (or domestic) matters than to public ones (see Broidy and Agnew 1997; Gilligan 1982; Heimer and De Coster 1999). Finally, because females are generally socialized to use peaceful means to resolve inter-personal disputes, they should be less likely than males to choose violent retaliation as a response to perceived affronts, and thus also be *less* inclined to retaliate in any form or *more* inclined to select a non-violent method for doing so.

The data broadly support Anderson's contention that the street code extends equally to criminally involved women – with our female sample members reporting numerous incidents of woman-on-woman retaliatory violence. Intriguingly, the modal reason for retribution they offered – whether they were victims or instigators of the retaliatory violence – was gendered in the sense that it revolved around disputes over a man. Like the male interviewees, the women interpreted this as disrespectful, and saw the need to use payback to restore their reputations. K-Loc described a typical incident. "This girl was messing around with my baby's daddy...and I found out...I see them together." K-Loc couldn't attack the woman then because her child's father was present. "But...eventually I seen her again, and we got to fighting...hard as we could."

As with the men, protection of family members was frequently cited as a reason for engaging in retaliatory violence. However, social networks are clearly gender-specific. In all cases save one, the women in our sample were retaliating against other women on behalf of female relatives. Miss Dee described standing up for her younger sister: "Some girls were talking bad to her because she is very educated and they were kind of jealous of her...when she got home [after being beaten up], she was crying...Me, her, and a couple of my other cousins, we went back up to the school the next day and you know we surrounded the girls, but they was too scared to do anything about it." Not only does this example emphasize the gender-specific nature of social networks in St. Louis, it also demonstrates that a potentially violent encounter can sometimes be resolved in a non-violent fashion. Female-on-female retaliatory encounters were far more likely to be resolved non-violently than male-on-male conflicts, at least in our data.

That said, Pumpkin described a series of violent retaliatory encounters directed at her younger brother's former girlfriend. Pumpkin's list of grievances against this woman was quite long, including the woman's unwillingness to contribute to household labor, being unfaithful to her brother, and stealing money from other people in the house. But the event that triggered Pumpkin to retaliate was when the woman called the police on her brother, against Pumpkin's expressed wishes. As Pumpkin explains:

> I just felt like she disrespected me when she brought the police to my house when I asked her not to. Now if he would have kicked her ass and she called the police, I still would have been upset, but I would have understood ... but she called the police just because she was mad, just cause he put her out ... I live in Section 8 housing and all I need is for the police to keep coming to my house and me and my kids are in the same predicament that she is, homeless. I can't have that, I can't have that.

In response, Pumpkin threw her out of the house, with the woman leaving in the company of the police. However, the woman returned to the same complex a few days later to stay with someone else in another apartment. This incensed Pumpkin, and as a result, she and a female cousin assaulted her:

> I was in my car, and I was coming out of the complex, and I saw her going the long way back from the store. 'Cause she could have come my way, and it would have been quicker. Me and my cousin was in the car and I saw her, but I drove past her ... I went and parked my car ... down the street from my house ... I walked up behind her, she didn't know I was behind her, and my cousin just grabbed her hair and I just started hitting her ... she didn't actually hold her down, she just grabbed her and then I hit her and then we both hit her. We just kept hitting her and she fell on the ground. She was kicking ... wasn't nothing she could do. We just

beat her up ... [I said to her,] 'Bitch, didn't I tell you not to call the police to my house? Now I'm gonna kick your ass for all the times I been wanting to kick you ass in the past.'

Asked why she chose to retaliate in the way that she did – that is, with measured, non-lethal violence – Pumpkin responded:

She don't own a car, she don't own shit and I ain't trying to go to jail for shooting nobody. I got kids to raise. But I beat her ass good ... I usually try to be more ladylike about the way I handle things, but I just felt like I had to kick her ass because she thought she was big and bad and she always ... make comments to my brother ... if your sister ever try to do something to me, I'm gonna kick her ass.

While the verbalized motive in this case centers on issues of respect – as do most of the retaliatory incidents in our data – here the respect concerns the domestic stability of Pumpkin's family, especially her children, in addition to her reputation. As predicted, then, the men in our sample typically talked about retaliatory events emanating from street-corner disputes, whereas the women more frequently identified incidents stemming from domestically oriented interactions.

Like the men in our sample, the women often had things stolen from them – theft being a fact of street life – and this caused some of them to retaliate against the person perceived to be responsible for the crime. K-Loc, for example, described how she responded to having her wallet stolen:

I asked everybody, [and] everybody like, 'No, I ain't seen it.' But for some reason when I asked [her sister's friend] ... it just seemed like she could have been lying ... so I hit her right in the mouth. Her mouth [w]as bleeding ... she hollering, acting the fool, and I'm beating her ass. [I] threw her out the door saying, "You ain't never coming in my house no more.

In a somewhat similar incident, Kimmy, who supported herself and her children through stripping and prostitution, had her purse stolen while she was servicing a client in a cocktail lounge bathroom. She assumed that one of her female co-workers, who had suddenly gone missing, had absconded with the purse; regardless, she had asked the woman to watch her money, and thus held her responsible for the theft. A week later, Kimmy received a call from her cousin, informing her that one of the woman's female friends was at a local convenience store. Kimmy immediately drove to the store and rammed her car into the other woman's vehicle. She then jumped out of the car and attacked the woman with a metal bar. Kimmy picks up the story:

> As soon as I seen her, I just hit [her] ass. I barely missed the first time...she done dropping her shit [purchases], like she can do some [damage]. I got this damn pole...my main thing is to kill her motherfucking ass...I was pissed...she knows who did it [the theft]. She knows that she was with them. When she see my face, she know what the hell I'm up there for." The fight ended when another store patron called the police and, at the time of our interview with her, Kimmy still had not located the person she suspected of stealing her purse. Nevertheless, she remained committed to getting revenge for the theft: "I cannot wait to get her...cause I'm gonna see her again, cause I got to go dance again. I'm gonna see this bitch, unless she skips town and not gonna dance no more.

A key difference between the retaliatory violence described by the men and women in our sample concerns the willingness to use firearms. While the men frequently reported using firearms in both lethal and non-lethal retaliatory encounters, only one incident of female-on-female retaliation involved a firearm. That incident involved Sugar, who was robbed and beaten at a bus stop. It took her over a month to track down the woman responsible for the crime, but having located her, Sugar and a female friend wasted little time in getting violent revenge. As Sugar describes it:

> I went around and I had me pistol. I had got a little .45. My partner went across the street, walked on the other side. She came

up and we just stood there and watched until she [the target] came to the back [where she kept a drug stash] and I upped it on her and I showed my face and said 'You remember me? You took all my shit'...[I said], 'Bitch, I want my shit! Then I'm gonna take your shit.' She looked over at me and I said, 'You remember me?' And I had put my gun like in the corner of her mouth...I gave her enough to not come back. She's sitting in a wheelchair now.

The modal form of female-on-female violence, however, involved fists and feet as weapons. Only four women mentioned the use of other weapons such as baseball bats or bottles. Seemingly, the women in our sample were neither frequently nor heavily armed, finding day-to-day objects to use as weapons when the situation called for it. In contrast, the men were less likely to report using such objects as weapons.

Compared with the men in our sample, the women were much more likely to draw on their peers to help them retaliate against someone, though not necessarily in a proxy fashion. The women never discussed hiring or asking another woman to exact vengeance on their behalf. Although in some cases the women did ask for *assistance* in carrying out an assault, in others their friends or family members just showed up to help during a retaliatory encounter. Indeed, virtually every incident of female-on-female violence in our data involved multiple participants on both sides.

## Female-on-Male Retaliation

Female-on-male reprisal should be the least common form of retaliatory aggression because, men are normally physically bigger and stronger than women, and more likely to be armed (Miller 1998). White and Kowalski (1994) have observed that if women perceive themselves as weak, they will avoid avenues of aggression and violence against men. Bolstering this observation, Miller (1998) found that female armed robbers generally avoid targeting males for this very reason. When victimized by men, then, women likely are dissuaded from seeking vengeance for fear of sparking counter-retaliation, or else to call on male associates to exact retribution on their behalf.

Of course, vengeance need not be "physical." Vandalism and burglary are just as readily available as predatory aggression to pay back someone who crosses you, but so also is sex – intercourse, for example, with friends or family members of the person who wronged you. Given that existing norms discourage females from resorting to violence, we might expect women to be more likely than men to rely on less violent or non-violent forms of retaliation (see, for example, Crick 2003; Crick et al. 2002).

Only five incidents of female-on-male retaliation were described by our respondents, and almost all of them involved non-violent forms of retaliation. When men wronged them, the women in our sample typically enlisted male peers to retaliate for them. Lady Ice, for example, told us: "We were at a club and one of the guys smacked me and I went out and I got [my male friends] and they came over and they beat the guy up . . . I got them and they came in and beat the other guy up pretty bad . . . I can't beat up [a guy] . . . I mean I could try, but I don't think I would win." And the following exchange between Sugar and one of the interviewers also taps into this dynamic:

| Sugar: | If a nigger [a man] step in – I got a whole lot of niggers – I know they can break him down. |
| Interviewer: | OK if a guy did it . . . then you get a guy to do it? |
| Sugar: | That's right. |

When retaliating for themselves against men, the women inter-viewed here usually sought revenge using non-violent means. Teaser, for example, was given gonorrhea by a man she was dating and, to get even, she and a female friend broke into the man's house: "[We] went ahead, took as much as we can, looked for his money, cause he usually have a safe in there. Tried to open the safe, couldn't get it open, so we just took the safe . . . [opened it later and got] $2000." Frizz used two different forms of non-violent retaliation to avenge her lover's infidelity. First, she turned the tables by having sex with other men to "spite him." Second, she damaged her lover's car by putting some "sugar and shit" in the gas tank. Obviously, neither act involved direct confrontation, perhaps because Frizz perceived herself to be smaller and weaker than the male who violated her. Certainly that is why Pumpkin, in the episode quoted next, decided not to retaliate against a man who publicly insulted her in a club:

> He was all up on me, you know, just all up on me breathing hard. He was just funky and I didn't like it. I was like damn, why don't you back up off of me. He got pissed: 'Look at this white bitch, bitch, fuck you, you ain't the shit, you ain't all that.' And I'm like, 'Damn, you must think I'm the shit, you must think I'm all that cause you the only one tripping.' I don't go nowhere thinking that I'm the finest thing walking the face of the earth or nothing like that, but he was just acting a fool with me. He said, 'All I want to do is get my dick sucked by a white bitch.' And that pissed me off. First of all, you don't talk to me like that, I'm a lady. No matter what I do, I'm still a lady. Second of all, who the fuck you calling white? . . . I wanted to [hit him], but he was too big . . . I wanted to bite him. I wanted to scratch him. I wanted to do whatever I could to him, but he would have kicked my ass.

## Gender and Retaliation in Perspective

The data presented here clearly demonstrate that retaliatory violence is gendered. Gendered perceptions of appropriate and inappropriate behavior serve as triggers for – and barriers against – retaliation. Men view violent retaliation as a key street survival tactic, deeply rooted in their identities *as men*. While this is not a new idea (see, for example, Anderson 1999; Hobbs 1994; Messerschmidt 1993, 1997, 2000; Polk 1994), the findings from this chapter enrich current understandings of the link between masculinity, the triggers of street violence, and the manner in which violent episodes play into men's perceptions of their own gender-role enactments and the gender enactments of others.

No prior research has addressed the issue of how men approach retaliation against women. As demonstrated in this chapter, when the males were confronted by another man, getting revenge was seemingly mandatory; when challenged by a woman, some of them indicated that they would let such actions slide, though most still saw the need to respond in some fashion. Men's use of retaliatory violence on the streets – regardless of the target's gender – is much more nuanced; it is framed within a complex set of contingencies that mediate male street violence. Clearly, even the extremely violence prone men in our sample are not always violent, and violence is not the sole resource used by them to construct masculinity on the streets.

Coupled with the results of other studies (Anderson 1999; Baskin and Sommers 1998; Miller 1998; Miller and White 2003; Mullins and Wright 2003), our data suggest a certain convergence of gendered actions within street life. The motivations for intra-gender retaliation seem very similar for men and women: the building and maintaining of street reputations. Our data clearly demonstrate that when a woman is disrespected or challenged by another woman, a desire for violent payback is common. Thus, as with women who enter masculinized space in other social arenas, women on the streets appear to have adapted to – and sometimes to have adopted – prevailing masculine attitudes and behaviors *vis-à-vis* aggression.

Although retaliatory disputes among both men *and women* typically revolved around issues of reputation, female retaliators attended to different constructions of reputation. For example, the women in our sample were more likely than the men to get involved in disputes over domestic matters. Moreover, our data indicate that while some women are drawn to resolve conflicts through violence, there is not the broad "masculinization" of female attitudes on the street that some scholars have suggested (for example, Baskin and Sommers 1998). In some ways, the reasons the women in our sample gave for their retaliatory violence were distinctly feminine (see also Miller and White 2003).

Few of the women we interviewed appear to have adopted masculine attitudes toward violence wholesale; compared with the men, they resorted to violence less frequently, with less severity, and were more likely to seek non-violent modalities of retaliation. That said, about a third of the women *did* offer up strongly masculinized attitudes toward violence, though they were a minority within our sample (which is remarkable since we purposely sought out such individuals). Even these women were hesitant to exact direct retribution against men who victimized them during the course of their street-corner interactions; we found that the women frequently took more indirect routes to accomplish their retaliatory goals. Prior work has shown that while women on the street corner face more obstacles to goal fulfillment than do men, they nevertheless are capable of negotiating these constraints in a complex fashion (for example, Maher 1997; Miller 1998; and Mullins and Wright 2003). Retaliatory violence is no different. For example, even though the women in our sample were hesitant to retaliate personally against men who wronged them, they had no qualms when it came to seeking out the help of allied men to exact payback on their behalf.

Whether – and, if so, how – our findings would have been different had we managed to recruit white male and female offenders who had experience with criminal retaliation is open to conjecture. Substantial research suggests that African-Americans who reside in extremely disadvantaged urban neighborhoods of the sort from which we recruited our sample – both males and females – are more likely than their white counterparts to legitimate the use of violence in certain circumstances (see Simpson 1991 for a review and discussion that highlights the role of gender in mediating the use of violence among African-Americans and whites). That being so, we might speculate that our findings are weighted toward more violent retaliatory responses to predation among both the men and the women, especially because negative perceptions of the criminal justice system may encourage many African-Americans to view violent self-help as their only realistic avenue of redress (Bailey and Green 1999). In general, however, we are in agreement with Covington (2003:274), who reminds us that ethnographic investigations focused exclusively on one racial group may tell us little about how that group differs from others: "After all, if we were to compare the most violent black bar patrons...to the most violent white regulars at a white bar... [which seldom is feasible in ethnographic investigations that, by explicit design, often privilege depth over scope], it might be difficult to discern any differences in their propensity for violence." The nature of our data make it difficult for us to draw the sort of comparisons needed to highlight potential intersectionalities of race, class, and gender within episodes of street retaliation (see Simpson and Elis 1995; West and Fenstermaker 1995). Rather, our data allow us to explore gender constructions on the streets of some of St. Louis's most disadvantaged neighborhoods and how those constructions mediate and express themselves during episodes of retaliatory violence.

The gendered patterns of vengeance in our data reflect the gender-segregated network characteristics of the streets in St. Louis, where there are fewer opportunities for inter-gender violence because men and women do not interact with each other very much in this context (see also Bourgois 1995; Maher 1997; Steffensmeier 1983). Thus, most of the episodes described in our data involve men retaliating against men or women retaliating against women. Indeed, it was only when we began to ask respondents directly whether they had ever retaliated against someone of the opposite sex that the cross-gender conflicts emerged. This social separation not only reduces opportunities for inter-gender retaliation, it also helps to maintain patriarchal values concerning the appropriateness of violence against women. Yet men on the streets redefine both women and violence in a highly situational way, and, just like women who penetrate the masculinized arenas of the business world, females who become deeply involved in street life may find their behavior judged by pre-existing masculinist ideals. As many of our male informants told us, when a woman "acts like a man" on the streets, she risks getting treated like one, despite sexist stereotypes that generally call for the protection and shielding of women from violence (see also Miller 2001).

Such contradictions highlight the dynamic and problematic nature of any gendered action or interaction. As many feminist scholars have emphasized, gender is neither static nor monolithic (see Connell 1987, 1995; Messerschmidt 1993; Miller 2002; Sim 1994; West and Fenstermaker 1995; West and Zimmerman 1987). The disagreements and contradictions in our data concerning women as acceptable targets of violence amply illustrate this – even within the description of a single retaliatory episode, the men sometimes demonstrated considerable ambiguity about whether or not their use of violence against the woman was appropriate in the circumstances (see also Miller and White 2003). Only by exploring these highly variant, wide-ranging discourses, can we come to a full understanding of the nuanced and complex effects of gender on violence.

A key question raised by our data concerns the perplexing finding that, in seeking to exact revenge, the men were much more likely than the women to resort to firearms, even though guns have been touted as substantial power equalizers on the streets. Other researchers have also noted that men are far more likely than women to use firearms, both in the general public and within the context of urban street life (see Miller 1998; Sheley and Wright 1995). General explanations for this difference have centered on men's socialization into gun use throughout their lives. In the context of street life, however, such an explanation seems unconvincing. Guns are ubiquitous in that environment and, though women are less likely than men to participate in streetlife, those who do are more routinely exposed to firearms. Perhaps women on the streets do not use guns because they are largely excluded from social networks that facilitate the distribution of illegal firearms. After all, these networks are dominated by men, as are the criminal networks that produce the cash necessary to purchase illicit firearms in the first place (see Bourgois 1995; Maher 1997; Miller 1998; Mullins and Wright 2003; Steffensmeier 1983).

It is striking that many of the men in our sample claimed never to use violence against women, despite the fact that numerous such instances were described to us (even by some of those who initially insisted they would never do so). A key aspect of hegemonic masculinity on the streets of St. Louis strongly discourages the use of violence against females – labeling it as "punk" behavior (a distinctly subordinate masculinity on the streets: see Connell 1995 for a full discussion of the nature of subordinate masculinities; see Mullins 2004 for a full discussion of masculinities on the streets of St. Louis). Thus, male offenders using the interview site as a location for masculinity construction may purposely have failed to mention episodes of violence directed at women. Alternatively, they may not have defined "lesser" assaults against women as violence that counts for the purposes of our research. When asked about retaliation, for example, the men may well have responded by drawing on cognitive categories derived in the context of street encounters, disregarding domestically based disputes.

Our findings hint at a decision-making process *vis-à-vis* retaliatory violence that is bounded by gendered considerations. We suggest that gender ideologies serve as a powerful mediator within offenders' retaliatory calculi. It is clear that some women on the streets of St. Louis have come to value violence as both an aspect of identity and as a tool of interpersonal interaction (also see Baskin and Sommers 1998). This is particularly reflected in the prevalence of female-on-female violence explored here. Yet, gendered understandings still bind women's decision-making processes when it comes to retaliating against men. When asked about using violence against males, for example, the women drew on stereotypical justifications for avoiding such confrontations (for example, men are bigger, stronger, or more vicious). Further, it is possible that the women's desire to retaliate against men was mediated by fear that doing so would undermine their feminine status and the protections that go along with it, thereby opening them up to undiluted depredations in the future. Men's decision-making processes are similarly bounded by gender. The demands of street masculinity often pushed the men in our sample toward violent resolution of challenges visited upon them by other males. When it came to retaliating against women, the innate contradictions of street masculinity lead the men either toward or away from violence depending on prevailing individual and situational factors.

In short, our data illustrate the strongly gendered nature of retaliatory violence on the streets of St. Louis. Men get locked into retaliatory cycles not only as an inevitable byproduct of their criminal embeddedness, but also because of the demands of actualizing a street masculinity identity. Women moving within these same criminal networks also find themselves ensnared by these broader rules of violent engagement, both as targets and as transgressors.

# FIVE

# Imperfect Retaliation

THE FORCE OF THE RETALIATORY IMPERATIVE might be likened to a rushing river, which, if blocked, readily finds an alternative course. In the real world, it is not always possible for victims to retaliate against the person who wronged them. The guilty party may be unknown, elusive, or possess too much coercive power. Or the victim may be too angry or otherwise impatient to delay action long enough to strike back against the wrongdoer. Wherever such conditions prevail, victims may be tempted to dissipate their mounting desire for retribution by attacking an innocent third party, thereby engaging in so-called imperfect retaliation.

Imperfect retaliation plays a crucial role in the contagious spread of inner-city violence. In attacking someone other than the guilty party, victims provoke additional disputes that cannot be justified by the logic of retribution. And because such attacks are unjustified, they are likely to provoke defiance on the part of the newly created victims, who end up wanting their own revenge. That revenge may be directed against their attacker, against the person who attacked their attacker (thereby setting in motion the train of events that led to their victimization), or against yet another innocent third party.

The existence of displaced aggression is well established in the social psychological literature (see, for example, Pederson et al. 2000). Its driving force is captured by the adage, "If you can't beat 'em, beat someone else." Substituting one target for another allows those who have been wronged to regain a measure of respect where it might otherwise be difficult or impossible to do so. The substitution is justified to the extent to which the displaced retaliatory attack is interpreted by others as a sign of the victim's toughness and competence – attributes likely called into question by the instigating affront (see Tedeschi and Felson 1994:366).

Recall, however, that imperfect retaliation typically is not the preferred response to a perceived violation, but rather the option of last resort. Failing to punish someone who has wronged you invites future insults from that person and others, who may interpret your inaction as cowardice. Targeted retribution advances punitive, deterrent, and pedagogical goals in ways that more diffuse forms of vengeance cannot, and that is why displaced retaliation is called "imperfect."

Imperfect strikes are by no means homogeneous. Some such strikes are *wholly* imperfect, involving victims who have nothing to do with the instigating violation and who are recognized by the grievant as having nothing to do with it. These victims are attacked for reasons of proximity, convenience, or opportunity. Other strikes are *relationally* imperfect, involving victims who have nothing to do with the instigating violation, but who are sufficiently close to the violator in relational space to justify an attack against them. Still other attacks are *marginally* imperfect, involving victims who are perceived by grievants to be involved in the violation – typically as accomplices, "set-up" persons, or associates of the wrongdoer – but whose culpability in the actual wrongdoing is not necessarily definitive or verifiable at the moment the strike occurs. Victims of wholly imperfect strikes are attacked because they are in the wrong place at the wrong time, victims of relationally imperfect strikes are attacked because they are kin, and victims of marginally imperfect strikes are attacked because they are guilty by association. Chapter Five explores displaced retaliation with this basic scheme in mind.

## Wholly Imperfect Retaliation

Culpability is central to the notion of justice, whether that justice is the official or the "street" variety. Punishment is only supposed to befall people who do something to deserve it. If this were not the way things worked, or if this were not the way people thought things worked, social order would be impossible (Lerner 1980). Even criminals understand the relevance and practical value of the so-called just-world hypothesis, as evidenced by the misgivings many express about victimizing so-called innocent people (see Sykes and Matza 1957). Wholly imperfect retaliation flies in the face of this philosophy, demonstrating that sometimes "getting back" – for example, money, pride, or self-respect – may be more important than "getting even."

Ironically, the logic of imperfect retaliation may be more readily apparent when the victim is innocent and attacked out of spontaneous rage. Striking first and thinking later is emblematic of victims lashing out in a state of intense anger, wherein the rage is so acute that delaying its discharge is impractical. In such cases, grievants attack any available target, disregarding the fact that it has little or nothing to do with the instigating affront:

> [S]o I was going to the bathroom [at a nightclub] and somebody pushed me on the back of my head and I didn't know who it was, so I hit the first person that I thought it was and this girl was totally innocent. Totally innocent, she was like, 'I ain't doing nothing, I ain't doing nothing.' 'It don't matter bitch, you was right there.' I don't know, I just snapped ... I didn't care ... I just hit the first person that I saw and then I found out the girl really didn't hit me, I don't know, it was like a reflex I guess ... it was like I wasn't in my right state of mind I guess, I don't know, I just had to hit the first bitch I saw, but she wasn't the one.
>
> [101 Hotamount]

Strikes displaced by the force of spontaneous rage rarely occur precisely because the actual violator is "right there" when the attack transpires. Striking a substitute makes little sense in such cases, and threatens to compound the humiliation of having been violated. That also is why reflexively displaced attacks, described in Chapter Three, tend not to occur, though the two modalities remain conceptually distinct. When retaliation is reflexively displaced, the violators are verifiable and present, but grievants elect instead to get even by taking it out on something or someone of value to them.

When retaliation is displaced but wholly imperfect, no such assumption is made, and misdirection results from unfocused anger.

Delays are a function of situational constraints that provide a reason and a rationale for striking imperfectly: The violator is not around or cannot be identified, the grievant needs to "take it out" on someone else, and that someone emerges only with the passage of time. Typically, the chosen target need not meet a specific set of inclusion criteria. More often than not, suitability appears simply to be a function of being at the wrong place at the wrong time. Thus, Player had little explanation as to why he and his associates assaulted a man walking through their neighborhood, subsequent to a drive-by shooting in which Player was a primary target, except for the fact that they could not locate the real perpetrators. They beat the man unconscious before stripping him and leaving him naked on the street. This man "didn't do nothing at all," Player revealed, but "you're mad [and] you want to get at anybody." TC launched a similar attack against a patron at a grocery store. Angered over his car being vandalized, his best friend's death, and an ongoing dispute with his baby's mother, he lashed out on a man who inadvertently bumped into him in one of the aisles. The man "just caught all of that," TC recalled. " I just turned around and just took all that out [on] him." Likewise, K Loc beat someone in a local store after an altercation at a local skating rink ended before she could strike back:

> One time me and this girl we had got into it. We had been skating. We got into it at the skating rink, she end up busting my head. The police came before we could even finish the fight or whatever, so when I'm there the first person I saw, anybody, walking down the street, it didn't matter, I was cursing and acting the fool, then I found one in the store. After I got by my house and I got in this store I see this lady, she just happened to be staring at me, pushed her right in her face hard as I could ... She said, 'What is going on' or whatever and I said to her, 'Don't worry about it.' Just acting the fool, trying to bust her head too, you know hard as I could ... I was angry from that person who busted my head in ... I had to release that because that would have just

wound me up. I wouldn't have been able to get no sleep or nothing ... [She was] the first person I came close enough to do something to.

If all a grievant seeks to do is to release pent-up anger by striking out, then almost anyone may substitute for an elusive violator. If the goal is to recoup material losses, the target must be chosen more carefully. That takes time. Though it remains true that the more time elapses between violation and response, the more difficult it is to claim that the act is one of imperfect retaliation, memories in street culture are long and the need to justify conduct is ever-present. As long as grievants can commit the attack under the vague auspices of moralism, the response remains one of balance-restoration rather than random malice.

Robbed of a pound of marijuana, Black and his partner were unable to locate the assailant, and decided to rob somebody else to recover their losses. Their victim turned out to be a patron of a local nightclub. "One night [we] saw him coming out the clubs," Black recalled. "Just rolled up on him ... My partner ran up on the side of the car and bust the side of the window out [and robbed him]." A month after being robbed of a necklace that belonged to his sister, Paris went to a notorious marijuana-dealing area to rob a dealer of his drugs. Although the intended offense had nothing to do with the loss of the necklace initially, all that changed when Paris spotted the dealer's gold Turkish chain. "I just walked up to him," he recalled. "He showed me his sack [of weed]. I showed [him] the gun. Said, 'I'll take that chain, you keep your weed' ... I needed the chain, that's what I really needed ... Cause I had to get my sister another chain ... I just got it for her."

The drug world is rife with wholly imperfect strikes, perhaps more so than any other illicit setting. The reason is partly practical and partly philosophical. Drug users and dealers are visible and accessible, they carry high-value contraband that can be readily converted to cash, they are deserving targets by virtue of wreaking destruction on persons and communities, and they are sufficiently numerous and geographically dispersed to offer a degree of anonymity to those who attack them. Many drug market participants anticipate such losses and "write them off" as a cost of doing business. And when losses are expected and perceived as non-traumatic, stick-ups often meet with minimal resistance. This fact, plus tough enforcement of gun laws in inner-city neighborhoods, helps to explain why many street corner drug dealers are unarmed, making them ideal targets for those seeking to recover losses sustained at the hands of another predator (Jacobs, Topalli, and Wright 2000):

> [Somebody stole] my pack ... two grand ... of crack ... I didn't know who stole it. I didn't know who stole it and I'm like I've got to find somebody, you know what I'm saying, so that I can get mine back ... I chose that guy cause he was the guy I saw that made the wrong move, that had hid his dope ... load of crack sitting over there in the hole ....In like, in an apartment building where they have driers, you know the vent that goes outside the house? ... He had it sitting in a drying vent ... and so I got it out the hole ... I lost two grand [but I] gained three grand [by stealing from him]!
>
> [Black-2]

> [Somebody burned me for $20 of crack] I couldn't find him. He's gone, he's outta there somewhere else. I can't find this guy ... so I retaliate by getting another guy that's selling ... So what I do later on that night is might pull up in a car ... We drove up to him. There weren't a lot of people out there. This was about around one or two in the morning. The guy still be out doing his thing, so we pulled up on him and said, 'Do you have anything?' He say, 'Yeah.' He [my partner] pull out about five or six one [dollar bills] with a five on top. He say give him a fifty [dollar-rock]. He [the dealer] give me a fifty, he [my partner] looking in my hand. I say, 'This do?' He say, 'Yeah.' So he pulls off.
>
> [Big C]

Wholly imperfect strikes need not necessarily be perpetrated against strangers. Sometimes grievants purposely substitute someone they know or know something about for the person who wronged them, using an accomplice to do their dirty work. Inside information offers a guaranteed and often substantial bounty that the grievant and accomplice can divide. And use of a surrogate ensures continued anonymity for the offender who organizes the scheme. If the set-up person is made to look like a victim too, the scam becomes even more convincing by conferring an additional layer of protection from scrutiny:

> Nigger stole my crack like two weeks ago. I've got to do something. Then another nigger says, 'I've got some motherfucking weed' ... and I'm saying, 'How much do you charge? 'Eight hundred.' So I'm like, 'Give me your number and I'll call you.' Called him later that night and I'm like, 'My boy [the co-conspirator] wants two pounds,' you know what I'm saying. It's like that so I go to my partner and say, 'I got a stealing going on man, let me have the [buy] money.' The [co-conspirator] ... that was my cousin, he gave me the [buy] money. He got $1,500 just so [the victim] could see the money. So I'm acting like I'm doing a transaction [with the victim] and [then I have my partner come] up to rob me. He gonna rob me and him. He robbed both of us. I'm like [to the mark], 'Goddamn, man we got robbed!' And all the time the dude he gone, the one who robbed us. My partner robbed us. He up on the curb waiting for me to rattle with him. Come on over to get the [buy] money back ... Get the weed, brought the weed down, sacked it up. I gave him like half a pound and had a pound and a half for myself ... once you break the weed down and sack it back up, you're gonna get like 200 sacks. That's two grand ... Pretty good for losing $100 [of crack].[1]
>
> [Black-2]

This scam was executed so effectively that Black-2 arranged a second transaction with the same victim four days later. Black-2 clearly intended to exploit this dealer until he "wised up":

> [I called him up,] 'Hey man, what's up man, I come up to your crib and do business, we ain't gonna meet each other on the street, [because] you know what happened.' 'Do the transaction at your crib.' ... He didn't suspect me at all cause he trust me like that,

[1] In all candor, Black-2 admitted he wasn't sure whether somebody had stolen his crack or whether he had simply misplaced it. The reason for his loss is less important than the imperfect mechanism he used to erase it.

you know what I'm saying. The game is not to trust people in this game. Once you let a person know that you trust them they're gonna get you, so I figured like this nigger trust me so I'm gonna keep getting this nigger till he figures it's me.

## Relationally Imperfect Retaliation

While wholly imperfect retaliation may allow grievants to vent their frustration or recoup lost assets, it often fails to convey the critically important message that they will not take violations lying down. Wholly imperfect strikes are not well-suited to sending this sort of message because the targets of such attacks had nothing to do with the instigating affront, and thus it is seldom apparent to them, or anyone else for that matter, why they were singled out. Perhaps this is why many grievants opt instead for relationally imperfect retaliation.

Relationally imperfect retaliation involves an attempt to get even via an attack on blood relatives of the violator. Such attacks require that grievants know the identity of the violator, suggesting that the strike is a substitute for direct retaliation in cases where the real culprit cannot be located or safely attacked, at least for the time being. The rationale behind the relationally imperfect strike is simple: "If I can't get you, I'm going to get someone near to you, as near as possible, so you know I am coming for you next." The assumption that such attacks will be communicated to the violator in question is clear, and message-sending is intrinsic to their appeal. "I know he [has] to find out," Goldie explained after attacking the brother of the man who shot him. "[A] friend might not know where he's [the violator] at or how to get in contact with [him] but I know your brother, I know your cousin, one of them would know." Such strikes may also help to flush out the violator. Letting people you care about take the punishment for you is cowardly and may turn members of your own side against you. In this sense, relationally imperfect strikes may be considered a crude form of blackmail.

Two months after being shorted $75 for a bag of marijuana, E had some of "his boys" break the legs of the brother of the man who fleeced him. "What other way you gonna make a person come back," E explained matter-of-factly. The violator reappeared two weeks later, ostensibly to forestall any additional attacks, at which point E had his henchmen assault him too. "Beat him down," E recalled without much emotion.

Unable to locate the man who robbed him of $1,000 worth of crack, Gerry went after the individual's family instead. "He wanted to hide," Gerry recalled, "so I had to get him one way or another." Fire-bombing the house belonging to the assailant's mother was his method of choice:

> Put some gas on his mama's house ... lit it up [with a Molitov cocktail] ... it burned good ... Premium unleaded. Oh yeah, don't use regular [gas]. Use premium. Higher octane. Burns better.

Hospitalized after being shot in the abdomen by someone he knew, Goldie went looking for the culprit, but ran into his older sibling instead. The sibling taunted Goldie. Though the imperfect strike might have taken place anyway, the taunts all but ensured its occurrence:

> After I got out of the hospital ... I just went out, you know, went out to see what the deal was by going to the same territory where everything happened ... The big brother laughed and joked, you know, 'Ah here he comes [Goldie], my little brother popped [shot] his punk ass ...' As I'm walking past I'm hearing all this, you know, I'm just walking ... I see his big brother and he's talking all this shit. 'Yeah my little brother shot him, his punk ass,' you know all that old crazy stuff. So I walk on round to the house, call my cousin, tell him, 'I need your burner [gun]', cause I don't have my burner. Walked back over there ... I just [started shooting at the guy] ... Hit him in the hand, and hit him in the leg.

Bishop exacted relationally imperfect retaliation on behalf of his sister, who had been beaten repeatedly by a man she called her boyfriend. One beating was so severe that, according to Bishop, it had turned her "orange." The violator also impregnated his sister and refused to take responsibility for the baby. Bishop actually retaliated directly against the man on several occasions – breaking his nose one time and his hip another. But the violator subsequently disappeared and Bishop, not satisfied that his message had gotten through to him yet, redirected his anger toward the violator's brother. Bishop claimed he was "cool" with the brother, but his need to communicate a message to the violator trumped any sympathy he may have harbored for him:

> [S]everal years ago he [the boyfriend] left the state. I had no idea where he is now, but he does have a brother who still lives in the neighborhood. His brother I've always been cool with, and [I] didn't have a problem with him, but I still had to have some kind of face. I had to save some kind of face, so we had his brother beaten up in clubs to try to get him [the violator] to come back ... We done it to him at least three times ... I basically just said [to the brother], 'You're no good if you can't take responsibility for your actions, so you're going to take responsibility for what [he] did. Until he shows his face and comes clean I'm gonna keep doing this to you.'

## Marginally Imperfect Retaliation

Attacks against kin are not always feasible, practical, or desirable. Grievants may not know the violator or may be unable to locate any of the responsible party's relatives. Alternatively, grievants may face situational constraints that make attacking the violator's kin difficult or impossible. Or, there may be a more logical and suitable target for them to attack – someone suspected to have been involved in the violation, even though that person did not actually brandish the weapon, throw the punch, or pull the trigger. For both punitive and deterrent reasons, it always is better for street offenders to retaliate against aggressors as directly as possible, but such strikes remain imperfect for lack of definitive proof that the person attacked is culpable for the violation in question. Suspicion is what drives these retaliatory attacks – a belief that the targeted individual

played a set-up, accomplice, or other associative role in the instigating affront.

Gerry was robbed of two ounces of crack and $2,000 cash while
having sex in a seedy motel room with a woman whom, he sur-
mised, had probably set him up. Two weeks later, he spotted the
woman at a local nightclub. He went out to the parking lot and
waited in his car. A friend lured the woman out of the club and over
to the vehicle. As she drew alongside, Gerry fired his weapon.
"Shoot through the window," Gerry recalled. "Bam it's over . . . she
can't come after me." Robbed, carjacked, and pistol-whipped by
three men, Paris could not determine the identities and whereabouts
of the perpetrators. However, he suspected his female companion of
collusion with the assailants. After his release from the hospital,
Paris and a cousin set out to find her:

> So we walked outside [the hospital] . . . and my cousin was like,
> 'Come here, come here.' And then they was like, 'Who the fuck
> did this shit?' I'm like, 'Some punk ass niggers . . . The trick [girl] I
> used to mess with set me up or what ever.' They was like, 'OK,
> we'll take a ride down there.'. . . [M]e and like two or three of my
> friends and my cousin, we went over there [to the girl's
> house] . . . Like three cars deep . . . I said [to the girls' mother]
> 'I was in that garage right there' and they all just got out the cars
> and walked up to the door and shit [and robbed me]. [H]er mama
> was talking some shit . . . My cousin got mad, I didn't do it, but
> my cousin got mad and just started shooting at the window.

How you categorize this marginally imperfect strike, and others like
it, ultimately depends on whether you believe the woman had something to do with the robbery. If she did, as Paris suspected, the strike
would indeed be marginally imperfect: The woman was instrumental
in getting Paris into a vulnerable position at a specific time and place
so that accomplices could enact the crime. If the woman played no
such role – and, for the record, both she and her mother reportedly
denied that this was the case – then the strike would be wholly
imperfect, retaliation exacted against an entirely innocent party. But
from the grievant's perspective, perception is all that matters, and

Paris was convinced that the woman was guilty. He reported that she once had offered to set-up a man for *him* to rob, but that he had refused to take her up on the offer. Paris also suspected that the woman had set him up for a separate robbery some months previously, because that crime was almost identical to the one described earlier.

Red turned his retributive attentions toward a marginally involved third party, though his suspicions were far from concrete. The man Red attacked had arranged a drug transaction between him and another man, a person Red did not know. This person sold Red $1,500 worth of what appeared to be crack, but actually was wax. Unable to locate the dealer, Red contacted the person who arranged the transaction – believing that he knew the so-called drugs were fake. This individual not only attempted to deny his involvement but tried to insinuate that Red himself was pulling a scam. Red retaliated against him following a heated verbal exchange:

[A]s soon as you get your stuff [powder cocaine] you go home and you rock your stuff up. If your stuff jump back you call the people and tell them it's cool. But if [it] don't come back or you don't get no response then you go back to the one who introduced you to the people. [That's what I did.] ... I'm like, 'Hey man, look John [pseudonym], you need to get back with Richard [pseudonym], man. Tell Richard that the stuff that he sold me is not about what it's supposed to be. It's wax.' 'Well how do you know that's right?' 'See man I'm trying to rustle this shit up and man this shit ain't coming back, it's wax.' Then I took it out and showed it to him and he's saying, 'Well how do I know you ain't switched on it?' So I'm like, 'Man, what do you mean?' Fifteen hundred dollars, you know that's a lot of money for me to be playing with. Then he tried to [walk off] ... I'm like, 'All Right.' Then about two or three minutes later he walked down the street and I was standing in the alley waiting on him ... and as he came out, I shot him ... He knew that stuff wasn't what it was supposed to be ... He knew it was bad ... all the time he knew it was bad.

Icy Mike had no specific knowledge of the identity or whereabouts of the person who shot his uncle, assassination-style, in the parking lot of a local Steak 'N Shake restaurant. The homicide occurred at 3 AM as his uncle was leaving work. There were no witnesses and nothing was taken, though the victim had valuables on him, including jewelry and the keys to his Cadillac parked just a few feet away. Icy Mike suspected his uncle's girlfriend was involved in the killing. She had stabbed his uncle in a domestic dispute just a few weeks prior to the shooting. Icy Mike was fairly certain that she had not pulled the trigger herself, but rather had put the killer up to the crime. When she showed up at the uncle's residence a week after the funeral, Icy Mike attacked her:

> [T]his bitch came to one of the family functions ... We were moving his apartment and cleaning out his shit. I just came up there and wanted to get a couple of shirts. I already got all the CDs and shit, they gave me shirts and shit, but she wanted to come up in there and I was just waiting for her ass to come up in them motherfuckers. So when she came up there I'm like, 'Bitch, what are you coming up in this motherfucker for?' Ain't nothing for you.' And the bitch got to yapping off her motherfucking mouth, that was good, that was all I wanted her to do ... She was saying, 'I loved him' and shit. I said, 'What do you mean bitch, you stabbed him the week before he got killed.' Fuck all that, I was so mad ... I smacked that bitch up. I dragged that bitch outside. She tried to swing on me, she told me she was going to get her cousin on me and shit, and while she was telling me that and I'm hitting her ass, she tell me that she's getting her cousin on me! I can't do nothing but increase the pain. So I slammed her ass into the car ... ain't nothing but fury and anger.

Icy Mike's uncertainty about the woman's role in the homicide was confirmed by his post-strike behavior, during which he "hung out" with his uncle's "homies" to elicit additional information that might exonerate her or more accurately, implicate someone else. "[A]ll I got to do is find out who he might have argued with, who he might have got into it with or whatever," Icy Mike explained. "If a motherfucker ... [was] arguing and shit [with my uncle] before [the murder] and I find out who it was or who was with him, they gonna get it." The fact that this might require an additional imperfect strike, marginal or wholly imperfect, did not seem to bother Icy Mike. Doing *something* was what mattered, and a probabilistic assessment of guilt provided justification enough. In a subsequent interview months later, Icy Mike not only expressed remorse about assaulting the uncle's girlfriend, but abandoned his plan to ferret out additional information after nothing of substance materialized. "I'm not hanging out with nobody [any more]," he remarked. The homicide case remained unsolved at the time of this interview, and at best was only marginally avenged.

Targets of marginally imperfect strikes need not be implicated as set-up people or accomplices. A mere associative role with the violator might be enough to make someone a target for revenge. Player thus launched a retaliatory drive-by shooting against several individuals, though only one of them had shot at him. The gunman was out and visible when Player and his co-offenders retaliated, but they made no effort to avoid hurting his associates. "[W]e didn't particularly care who was out there," Player recalled, "the guy ... was out there ... he's just a single person and you got about seven or eight people standing out there ... we crept down there and licked them motherfuckers ... Let it out." How the violation itself unfolds – messily and with little concern about collateral damage – may play a role in shaping the imprecise nature of the attacks that follow. "[W]hen he [the violator] was shooting," DL recalled impassively, "my little brother just happened to get hit. He [the shooter] didn't care ... [so when we went back], anybody that out there just got hit."

Smoke Dog was attacked by a man with a Tech-9 assault weapon after he shot the same man in retaliation for slapping his mother. Seeking vengeance, Smoke Dog grabbed an S-K assault weapon and drove to the attacker's neighborhood. Unable to find the man who had attacked him, he unloaded the 65-round clip anyway, targeting individuals he associated with the attacker. "I don't have bunk missions" [street slang for sorties without purpose] he insisted. "Some of 'em [the violator's associates, who may or may not have been involved in the shooting] was out [on the streetcorner],

but not the one I'm looking for ... [so] I got to shootin' at anybody ... Boom! Boom! Boom! Boom! Boom! Boom! Boom! Boom!
Boom! Pow! Pow! Pow! Pow! Pow! Pow! I shot all 65 of [those
bullets]."

Smoke Dog generalized guilt even more inclusively in a second,
unrelated incident – robbing any perceived "partner" of the man
who had robbed him. He retaliated time and again, his rage not
satiated by a long series of marginally imperfect strikes – ostensibly
because he did not get the person who had actually wronged him.
Attacking the violator's associates was the best he could do, something he did in almost binge-like fashion:

I went there [to the neighborhood from which the violator
operated]. I saw one of the little cats who was out there with the
dude, right, so I'm like, 'Well, where is he?' I'm hollering at him.
But I ain't telling him the boy robbed me ... I'm like, 'Where your
partner is?' He's like, 'You just find out, he's somewhere.' So I'm
like, 'OK, you give me what you got!' You dig? For real! I told
him like, 'Give me what you got.' Robbed his ass [of $100 cash
and $50 of crack]. Went down the street, motherfucker like, went
to this house where they sell weed. I go knock on the door and rob
every motherfucker in there. Knocked on the door and robbed
every motherfucker in there. Dude opened the door. When I
knocked on the door ... soon as this motherfucker open the door,
we just stuffed some bitches [guns] in his face and told him,
weren't nobody there but him and his gals and two little babies. I
ain't no baby killer, I ain't [indecipherable] no babies – I got
babies. I'm just like, 'Give me what you got', and he had all crack
in that motherfucker, I'd say about seven ounces of crack ... in
the freezer ... These are his [the violator's] homies, all homies. So
I'll rob every motherfucker out there. We just chilled for a little
minute, hung out, smoked some blunts. About two nights later
[we] was back on that motherfucker [street] again in a stolen car.
Just robbing every motherfucker ... Back on the same block,
robbing every motherfucker ... We walked down the street,
robbed every motherfucker ... We caught them in a dice game.
All the cats surrounding that dice game, shit, we just walked up to
them and showed them the shooters [guns]. My little homie he

had the motherfucker, he was just waiting on me to up something, showed them the shooters, so he ain't saying too much ... 'Everybody get up!' My other homie come out. 'Get up!' Every motherfucker getting up. 'Empty your pockets!' Drop on the ground ... About eight guys. Dropped on the ground ... Took everything that was out. Even their rings, straight on. [One guy] got some nice shoes on his feet, the size I wear. I ain't really on to taking motherfuckers' shoes off, but I took them just to piss him off. I end up throwing them away or give them to one of my little homies or something ... One tried to run and I hit his ass [shot him] ... motherfucker shouldn't have tried to run.

The importance of Smoke Dog's story lies in both what it encapsulates and what it symbolizes. Far from eliminating grievants' rage, imperfect strikes may intensify it. The realization that the person who actually wronged them remained unavenged almost inevitably continued to haunt the respondents who had to settle for imperfect retaliation, stoking an anger that only a direct attack could dissipate. "[I]t ain't even," Goldie proclaimed after attacking the brother of the person who robbed him. "I want him [the specific violator]." "No way [are we] even." Moon echoed this sentiment following a retaliatory drive-by shooting directed against associates of the person who shot his uncle in the stomach with a .38, narrowly missing Moon himself. "[It's not even] cause we ain't got the one that shot us ... [I]f I see [the violator] on the street he's done. Put it that way." Though Big C made a lucrative score during the imperfect strike he committed in retaliation for a drug deal gone bad, he still was "gonna beat [the violator's] motherfucking ass and rob him."

Likewise, the excessively violent retaliatory strike that Red launched against one violator while looking for someone else did nothing to moderate his desire for revenge against the second individual. The "same day I shot the dude [the violator he chanced upon]," he told us, "I rode around all night [looking for the other guy]. I think I rode two days up and down ... It [shooting the first violator] got a little frustration off, but it didn't get all the frustration off, because ... that was just one. [It's] stuck in your brain, you want *him* [emphasis added] ... " Bishop's frustration only grew after assaulting the brother of the man responsible for beating and impregnating his sister, so much so that he feared what he might do when and if he came into contact with the violator again. "Getting his brother made it even more frustrating because it wasn't him," Bishop explained, "and until I can settle up with him ... [it's an] impasse ... to this day if I see him, I mean he could walk into this room right now, I'd just break a chair over his head ... That's what's scaring the hell out of me, man. Cause I know that if I see him, I'm gonna get taken over by rage."

Central to most tales of vengeance is a "love of precision" and the singular pursuit of "symmetry and closure" (Barreca 1995:82). In some cases, violators will never be identified or located, and the rage they inspired will incubate indefinitely. *Direct* retaliation may be as excessive as it is, at least in part, because imperfect reprisal is an unacceptable punitive replacement. People keep "ledgers" of the wrongs committed against them, and the accumulation of una-venged wrongs figures into shaping the reactions for wrongs that are repaid (see Tedeschi and Felson 1994:353–4). When the certainty of direct punishment is less than absolute, the severity of punishment automatically rises to compensate for it (see Posner 1980). If grievants displace their anger from those they cannot retaliate against to those they can, direct retaliation may actually have an imperfect component to it.

### Imperfect Retaliation and the Search for Justice

There are two broad philosophical rationales for punishment, whether that punishment is "street" or "state." The first holds that sanctions are "forward-looking" – that the primary objective of sanctions is to bring about social good by deterring, incapacitating, or rehabilitating the rule-breaker, by educating the populace about boundaries of acceptable behavior, by providing comfort for those who have been victimized, and by offering satisfaction for onlookers who think that retribution is right (Moore 1993). The second holds that sanctions are "backward-looking," – necessary only to pay back wrongdoers for what they have done. Deservingness lies at the heart of both rationales, but especially the second: People are punished "because, and only because, [they have] performed a culpable wrongdoing" (Kershnar 2001:17). On purely retributivist grounds, imperfect retaliation cannot be justified because, by definition, the individual targeted is not directly responsible for the violation.

But justice is perceptual, and imperfect strikes occur in the *name* of justice even if they are objectively unjust. Wholly imperfect strikes are "just" inasmuch as targets are tarnished in some fundamental way: Innocent of the violation in question, the target may be guilty of other reprisable offenses and therefore bear a kind of collective liability for creating the possibility of such attacks (for example, drug dealers). Relationally imperfect strikes are "just" by way of a transitive attribution of guilt: The targets are not culpable, but someone close to them is, thereby rationalizing the attack. Marginally imperfect strikes are "just" to the extent that the target played a role in the violation in question, however tangential this role may be. Though this knowledge is not necessarily definitive or verifiable at the moment the strike occurs, the attribution of vague responsibility is all that matters.

Obviously, any provocation that infuses imperfect strikes with higher moral purpose increases the odds of displaced retaliation. At least four respondents – Goldie, Red, K Loc, and TC, and possibly a fifth (Icy Mike) – described what social psychologists have called "triggered displaced aggression." Its defining feature is "the provision of a second provocation, a *triggering event*, by the target of displaced aggression" (Pederson et al. 2000:914, emphasis in original). The second trigger is often trivial – a stare, a bump, an offhand insult – acquiring significance only when viewed against the backdrop of the initial wrong. Primed by the initial violation and blocked from discharge, anger is released at the expense of someone believed to have committed a second wrong, albeit a minor one by comparison with the original affront. As a result, the force of the displaced aggression is often strikingly disproportionate to the violation, but this is understandable given that the first affront is the one that is really being "punished."[2] Through such actions, grievants seek to restore a sense of generalized reciprocity, though the resulting eqilibrium typically is both temporary and illusory.

This last point is important because it underscores the inherently ambivalent quality of imperfect retaliation. It is best considered an interim procedure – not optimal but satisfying given the alternative of doing nothing (see, for example, Simon 1979). Not all grievants will choose it, and even those who find it acceptable in some circumstances may not in others. Attacking someone closely associated with the violator likely represents the preferred form of imperfect retaliation because the actual violator almost certainly will hear about it and may be drawn out into the open. Nevertheless, it remains inferior to the direct strike. Whether the shortened distance to the desired retaliatory target makes vengeance any sweeter (or at least "less sour") is a separate issue, though a bad taste will likely linger until true symmetry is achieved.

Given the role of retaliation in the diffusion of violence, what happens after an imperfect attack is perhaps as important as what inspires it in the first place. Victims of displaced retaliation may well conclude that they have been singled out for no reason. This will almost invariably be the case for wholly imperfect attacks, but probably also for some marginally and relationally imperfect ones – at least until more complete information about the reason for the strike surfaces. Given that overlapping lifestyle and activity patterns disproportionately select other offenders for victimization, additional conflict is likely irrespective of that inspired by the defiance and emboldening effects described early in the chapter. This conflict derives from principles of compensatory justice, which suggest that when people suffer an undeserved punishment, they are entitled to

---

[2] The case of Bernard Goetz is perhaps the most compelling illustration of triggered displacement. Mugged on a New York subway, Goetz subsequently armed himself. Two years after the mugging, four young subway riders approached Goetz with what he perceived to be menacing intentions. Goetz shot all of them, one in the back, as he attempted to flee. Goetz admitted that he was "out of control" and that he behaved like a "cornered rat," but the jury was sympathetic – exonerating him of all charges except one, illegal possession of a firearm (see Baron, Forde, and Kennedy 2001; Marongiu and Newman 1987).

commit an affront equal to the punishment received. They are "owed" it, and anyone can repay the debt, not just the person who committed the violation. Kershnar (2001:6) illustrates this principle:

> Jones has just served five years in prison. His government convicted him of a rape he did not commit ... Jones claims that he is owed compensation for his unjust punishment. The standard to which compensation should conform is restitutition which, in Jones's case, equals five years of freedom from incarceration. Jones then commits a rape and claims his compensation in the form of his not being punished for his act since the usual incarceration equals the compensation he is owed.

Preliminary evidence suggests that the belief that one is due a "free crime" may be particularly strong among victimized street criminals (Jacobs, Topalli, and Wright 2000). If this is true, what seem to be otherwise unprompted acts of crime and violence may really be imperfect retaliatory strikes in disguise. The unprecedented levels of urban violence in the late 1980s and early 1990s can be attributed at least in part to the need of frustrated grievants to get even at someone else's expense (see also Goldstein 1985 on the concept of "systemic violence"). How much instability, and how destructive its consequences, depends on whether any deterrent effects accrue to such strikes at the same time. The two forces are countervailing, but by no means mutually exclusive. Consider the following.

Urban crime networks are dense and news travels fast, so in the case of marginally and relationally imperfect retaliatory attacks, violators will almost certainly hear that someone close to them has been retaliated against. This may dissaude them from committing future violations, especially if associates more closely monitor those individuals' behavior to avoid incurring a liability that they might have to repay (see Posner 1980:84). In at least some marginally imperfect strikes, the violator may actually be present when the attack occurs, providing direct experience with punishment, and possibly an additional source of deterrence. General deterrence hinges on the extent to which potential violators with no situational or relational affiliation to the violator hear about the retaliatory strike and thereby are inhibited from transgressing the grievant. At a minimum, this requires recognition that the act in question is retaliatory; without such knowledge, it looks like nothing more than another senseless crime – theft and violence for the sake of theft and violence, which may inspire attempts to put the "violator" in their place.

Recent increases in the density of street criminal networks seemingly enhance the prospects for general deterrence. In response to zero-tolerance policing, offenders have aligned themselves more exclusively along kinship and filial lines – with people they know and trust – to increase barriers to penetration and thereby make arrest and prosecution more difficult (Curtis and Wendel 2000). When networks become more insular, they become more cohesive, and cohesiveness accelerates information flow. Word about retaliatory strikes – who committed them, who was targeted, and what punishment was inflicted – travels more rapidly through the grapevine, priming the process of vicarious learning. Inasmuch as information often gets distorted and sensationalized as it is told and retold, the deterrent effect may be still further amplified. Whether it is sufficient to "cancel out" the conflict-spreading potential of imperfect retaliation is unclear, but the possibility is intriguing.

# SIX

# Retaliation in Perspective

CRIMINAL RETALIATION CANNOT BE understood fully without reference to the socio-cultural context that provides much of the motivating force for its exercise. At a minimum, that context shapes offenders' judgments about what constitutes a meaningful affront, how serious it is, and what action should be taken in response. The underworld of urban street criminals is characterized by "aggressive regulative rules" (Baron, Forde, and Kennedy 2001) that promote a normative environment in which everyone is hypersensitive to inter-personal slights, however minor they may appear to outsiders. Small provocations produce disproportionately intense reactions because street identities are objectively shallow, based almost exclusively on the respect actors can command in inter-personal encounters. By refusing to take a perceived slight "lying down," and striking back effectively, offenders earn "street credibility" and a trans-situational identity as someone not to be crossed.

In the extra-legal setting of the urban street corner, respect is all about toughness, and toughness flows from the ability to inspire fear. Fear has currency that transcends the cathartic or the sensual; it allows you to get what you want from others while protecting yourself from the advances of would-be predators. To inspire fear is to create an illusion of dire consequences. This is not to deny the reality of objective threat, but rather to suggest that human beings seldom assess risk dispassionately. The tendency for people to focus on the perceived magnitude of potential consequences, as opposed to the statistical probability of suffering those consequences, is well recognized. Street criminals capitalize on such distortions to construct a fearsome persona, using retaliation to advertise their capacity for crippling violence while counting on human nature to amplify the link between observed severity and perceived certainty.

Street retaliation is about more than responding to discrete violations. Some transgressions may be worse than others, but all criminal retaliation is driven as much by a particular violation's deeper symbolic meaning as by the actual harm that violation causes. On the street, any affront, however petty, undermines your personal security by exposing weakness to others. The principal way to repair this reputational damage is to strike back.

Criminal retaliation derives from more than a simple search for security, however. Street actors in general, and street criminals in particular, are judged by their demonstrated – and highly individual – ability to make things happen. Those who successfully slough off the mundane concerns of ordinary citizens in favor of a life "shot through with action" (Katz 1991:297) have the highest status. Street status is pursued through, among other things, desperate partying, gambling, ostentatious consumerism, and sexual conquests (Wright and Decker 1997), but the most prestige is reserved for the so-called "bad ass" who responds to any affront without regard for the consequences. Retaliation proclaims an abiding unwillingness to let somebody dominate you, and on the street-corner, few actions broadcast a more sweeping message about who you are and what you represent. Striking back against those who cross you affirms that you are "bad," and badness is what street identity is all about. "To be 'bad' is literally to be good: [It] is inextricably bound up with the premium put on masculinity, physical toughness, and street wisdom ... To be bad is the main criterion for status [on the streets]; its primacy cannot be overemphasized" (Macleod 1987:26; see also Shover 1996).

Being bad has an intrinsic appeal that reinforces the inherent satisfaction derived from "getting your own back." Vigilante justice is what social order used to be about. The rise of formal law and law enforcement may have helped social systems to stabilize – by sublimating the desire for personal vengeance among the law-abiding – but remnants of a deep-seated retaliatory instinct continue to shape much human conflict:

> Revenge is as human and as inevitable as hunger ... The impulse we have to restore our self-esteem when we feel someone has deliberately taken it from us is one of the most universal and reliable ones in human nature ... Feelings of revenge aren't governed by logic or controlled by intellect, but instead emerge from the most buried parts of yourself, the parts we are least comfortable acknowledging.
>
> Barreca 1995:12

The sensual appeal of personal retaliation is especially strong in the context of the urban street corner – a world largely beyond the law. In this context, grievants act as both judge and jury, designating sanctions and the conditions under which those sanctions are imposed. In most cases, grievants themselves deliver the prescribed punishment. Few activities permit a more complete and visceral demonstration of personal competence. The personal danger inherent in retaliation is embraced to manifest transcendent powers of control (Katz 1988). In the process, grievants come to grips with the "brute being" that anchors their existential self (Adler 1985), displaying fearlessness in the face of threat and an appetite for threat itself (cf. Jacobs 2000). The way in which grievants embrace danger suggests that something far more serious than simple justice is at stake. Violations threaten identity, and threats to identity represent a fundamental challenge to personal autonomy, which is what gives identity its life force. Autonomy represents the essence of who people are and how they define themselves, especially in street culture, where any kind of subordination is anathema (Shover 1996). Retaliatory strikes, especially those that are excessive, proclaim that autonomy will be protected and advanced at all costs. Notions of re-establishing equilibrium are jettisoned in favor of uncontested victory. To win, you must wipe out any trace of the subordinating residue that tarnished you. Violators must be vanquished because their obliteration ensures your elevation. As the wrongdoer is brought down, the grievant is resurrected (Ripstein 1997:101).

The rationality of such actions is open to debate. It seems perfectly reasonable to want to retaliate against someone who has wronged you, especially where access to the formal legal system is blocked, but rational punishment typically is scaled to the magnitude of the harm intended or done (Sarat 1997). Notwithstanding the fact that symmetrical sanctions are seldom regarded as sufficiently punitive in street culture, there is a certain existential logic to excessive reactions that betrays their core rationality. Choice is about more than dispassionately balancing objective factors in a decision matrix to reach a "logical" course of action. It is subject to deeper phenomenological forces that can imbue seemingly senseless acts with profound transcendental meaning. The "sense" in such acts becomes apparent only when viewed in relation to the actor's immediate phenomenological environment. Thus:

> [A] 'wanton' act of smashing a window might actually be committed for the fun of it or the excitement of running away afterwards. A man might brutally beat his wife, not simply because he is a violent thug, but because this is the easiest way of getting her to do what he wants. 'Senseless' acts of ... gang violence might confer considerable prestige on the perpetrators among their peers. The term joyriding accurately conveys the main reason why cars are stolen – juveniles enjoy riding around in powerful machines.
>
> Clarke and Cornish 2001:24–5

Retaliation in general, and retaliatory excess in particular, permits grievants to "let go" – of anger and frustration – completely and deliciously, at the expense of someone who has wronged them or, in the case of imperfect retaliation, a close punitive substitute. This exercise is as emotional as it is practical. Violations cut to the core of who street offenders are and how they perceive themselves. Criminal victims want violators to pay. They want them to hurt. They want violators to think about the strike long after it happens. There is more than justice at stake; identity hangs in the balance.

The discharge of rage is liberating, even sensual. "Revenge, like illicit sex, rich foods, ornate decorations, extravagant cars, and hundred-dollar haircuts ... [is] desirable because it's ... extreme [and] unnecessary" (Barreca 1995:34). Certainly, the cathartic release of anger is a benefit of criminal retaliation separate from any cash or goods recouped in the process. Arguably, it is more valuable than any resulting cash or goods because its locus is purely cognitive and therefore not reducible to objective measurement. Such benefits speak to the essence of rational choice.

## The Formalization of Informal Justice

One wonders whether the sensual appeal of street retaliation has anything to do with its growing – and ironic – absorption into the *official* management of crime. Few would deny that justice has become more humane in the last 250 years, but many complain that with that humanity has come too much leniency. In response, authorities are lobbying for – and securing – harsher, more certain punishments. Mandatory minimum penalties, sentence enhancements, and "three-strikes you're out" laws have come to dominate criminal jurisprudence. Incarceration for incarceration's sake is no longer tough enough. Privileges (for example, TV, exercise and weight-training, recreational time, educational programs) are being scaled back in prisons and jails across the United States and elsewhere. Administrative segregation is all the rage. So are hard-core boot camps and no-frills prisons run by private corporations whose profit-motivated cost cutting has created conditions not unlike the post-World War II Soviet gulags (see Dyer 2000). Probation and electronic monitoring, once championed as alternatives to incarceration, have become penalties in their own right, often for minor violators who previously would have attracted no criminal sanction (Miller 1996). Some policymakers even have suggested replacing incarceration, for at least some offenders, with corporal punishment. For all intents and purposes, this is street justice, only formalized.

The "War on Crime" metaphor that drives all of these so-called get tough initiatives is in itself revealing. Designed to "impassion the population with a desire for vengeance" and to engender a "belief that vengeance is an acceptable solution to human problems," the metaphor encourages ordinary citizens to "experience resentment toward crime and criminals [and to] succumb to the passion to express that resentment by 'fighting fire with fire'" (Williams 2002:106). The fact that the metaphor works is attested to by the rapid spread of laws that allow citizens to carry concealed firearms – a clear attempt to disperse the potential for retaliation throughout the law-abiding population.

That said, the notion of "legalized revenge" rests uneasily with many people and even more so among philosophers and pundits. It almost inevitably "resounds as an indictment, embodying ... the general conviction that vengeance has no place in modern jurisprudence" (Jacoby 1983:114). Payback is personal, law is social, and it is the "removal of private animus ... that distinguishes the rule of law from the rule of passion" (Jacoby 1983:115). One of the reasons that retaliation disappeared as a modal form of dispute resolution is because it had a tendency to intensify disorder. With law came standardized social control, making "of its jurisprudence a keystone in the bridge a community builds from anarchy to order" while protecting "the stability of a society by providing systematic channels [and] measured recompense" (Seton 2001:89).

Even the most vociferous of critics, however, inevitably realizes that formal sanctions remain distinctly retributive irrespective of political climate. If this were not so, everyone would be "entitled to one free crime" (Jacoby 1983:274). Society wants rule-breakers to pay regardless of future wrongdoing, victim compensation, or just about anything else. This payment must be personal and sufficiently painful to replace what was "taken." Only by doing so can punishment restore the "sense of physical and emotional integrity ... shattered by [the violation]" and provide "assurance to the victim that the [violation] was an exception to the rule, a violation of an order that society is determined to uphold" (Jacoby 1983:298). Informal street justice cannot do this because aggrieved parties act on behalf of themselves, not the collective. However, public punishment must retain enough private zeal to be just: "The absence of sufficient retribution becomes a twofold attack on the sense of moral order that most people require to sustain their existence" (Jacoby 1983:299), in the first instance by failing to meet the obligation for reciprocity, and in the second by putting the rights of the offender ahead of society's debt to the victim.

If a desire for vengeance is a fundamental human impulse, and social-control institutions reflect this impulse in their sanctions, some degree of retribution will be unavoidable in the imposition of official penalties. The question is whether legal institutions magnify the impulse's destructive consequences by formalizing it, or whether their failure to do this would undermine the "bite" that punishment needs to be just. Tough sanctions may appear unseemly or uncivil, but lenient punishment threatens an even greater collective cost. As Supreme Court Justice Potter Stewart cogently remarked:

> The instinct for retribution is part of the nature of man, and channeling that instinct in the administration of criminal justice serves an important purpose in promoting the stability of a society governed by law. When people begin to believe that organized society is unwilling or unable to impose upon criminal offenders the punishment they 'deserve,' then there are sown the seeds of anarchy – of self-help, vigilante justice, and lynch law.
>
> Justice Stewart, Furman v. Georgia,
> quoted in Sarat 1997:171

## Bringing Formal Justice to the Streets

For street offenders victimized by other criminals, these debates are academic at best. Practically speaking, these offenders have little or no access to the stabilizing forces of the formal legal system. As a result, the underworld of street crime is highly volatile, and it will likely remain so unless criminal victims are granted the same benefits of formal justice available to law-abiding citizens.[1] Criminal victims

---

[1] The remainder of this paragraph and the three paragraphs that follow have been adapted from Rosenfeld, Richard, Bruce A. Jacobs, and Richard Wright 2003. "Snitching and the code of the streets," *British Journal of Criminology* 43:291–309, copyright © 2003. Reprinted with kind permission of Oxford University Press.

may appear to be undeserving of the law's protection, but the result of withholding it from them is that many will resort to informal methods of dispute resolution. The resulting crime and violence are not easily contained, threatening populations far removed from the original disputants.

Altering the relationship between the authorities and street offenders could help change this state of affairs. The police would do well to begin to treat the victimization of criminals by fellow lawbreakers as the serious problem that it is, and not as something to be tolerated or sometimes even encouraged. Moreover, authorities should make every effort to protect offenders who pass information to them from being identified as "snitches" by other criminals, something that seldom happens nowadays. Any improvement in the relationship between police and criminals will happen slowly and piecemeal, but we know that change is possible because it already has begun to occur, albeit incrementally, in the relationship between the police and one category of offenders: sex workers (Jenness 1993).

Pressures from the women's movement over the past two decades have made the police more responsive to sex workers' reports of criminal victimization. The police are now more likely to treat prostitutes as genuine victims and credible complainants when they report a crime. Nothing prevents police from granting other street offenders the same opportunities for legitimate access to the law. But, so far, nothing impels the police to do so either. No social movement has taken up the cause of legal access for street criminals. However, the prisoners' rights movement conceivably could move in that direction, especially as prison-to-community "re-entry" programs gain momentum (Travis, Solomon, and Waul 2000).

It is not farfetched, then, to propose that the kinds of political pressures and social conditions that altered relations between the police and sex workers could lead to expanded legal access for street criminals. Criminals, virtually by definition, will never have the legal rights and opportunities of non-criminals, and the police are unlikely to grant victim status and expanded legal access to the most violent street offenders. But the bulk of street crime consists of property offenses, simple assaults, and low-level drug dealing. People who engage in these illegal activities on a regular basis make up a disproportionate share of crime victims. Widening their access to legal resources could reduce their reliance on informal means of dispute resolution, and help contain the spread of contagious violence. At a time when people who previously opted not to bring disputes to the attention of formal authorities are now doing so in droves, where litigiousness is at all-time high, and where ordinary citizens feel a sense of legal "entitlement" unprecedented in the modern era (Merry 1990), this proposal does not seem unrealistic.

But the difficulties inherent in making formal justice available to criminal victims are nothing compared with getting them to take advantage of it. Legal mobilization requires that offenders grant legitimacy to the law and its representatives. They must, in other words, develop a "legal consciousness" that allows them to see the law as something feasible and practical to enlist. As Merry (1990:37) observes, "Before a person can bring a problem to [the authorities], he or she must conceptualize it as something that 'law' ... can help ... Behind the recourse to [authorities] for various kinds of problems lies an image of the law as appropriate and helpful." Serious street offenders, however, seldom hold the criminal justice system in such high regard.

Respect is the bedrock on which legitimacy rests. No institution will be regarded as legitimate if the power it represents is not respected. By breaking the law, street criminals demonstrate that whatever respect they may have for the criminal justice system is overridden by prevailing situational conditions, but, truth be told, few of them had much respect for that system to begin with. Putting it bluntly, most serious street offenders despise formal authority and all it stands for. Such contempt, especially for the police, cannot be erased or even reduced through simple policy changes. Hatred for the police is embedded in the very fabric of street culture. The police are very much aware of this. They see "it in the cold stare[s] they get [as they patrol the streets] – 'eyefucking,' as [they] call it (Simon 1991). They ... see it in the contempt and disrespect with which they are often treated by the public (Black 1971). And, above all, they ... see it in the lack of cooperation that greets their efforts to solve crimes" (see, for example, Canada, 1995:128–130; quoted in Cooney 1998:123). Get-tough, zero-tolerance strategies exacerbate the enmity that many offenders feel toward the police. If authorities continue to be defined in this way on the street, the perceived availability of law will always be low, and offenders' reliance on self-help will remain correspondingly high.

The stigma attached to snitching remains an even more persistent deterrent to criminal victims' attempts to mobilize the criminal justice system on their own behalf. On the street, cooperating with the police, even if only to report being victimized, not only labels you a snitch, it also makes you look weak, and weakness invites further victimization. Seeking the protection of the law "is to confess publicly that you have been wronged," an act that places you in great jeopardy, "a jeopardy from which the 'satisfaction' of legal compensation at the hands of a secular authority hardly redeems" (Pitt-Rivers 1966:30 quoted in Cooney 1998:122). Even if the police could be contacted with impunity, the premium that street culture places on self-reliance and its reputational link to respect would probably undermine the legal mobilization option. Law "availability" means nothing if law is not perceived to be viable to use, and on the street it simply is not acceptable to rely on external authorities to do your bidding for you.

The street criminal underworld is unlikely ever to enjoy substantial stability unless or until effective *localized* systems of dispute resolution develop. The problem is not so much one of conflict – every social system that involves human beings has conflict (Cooney 1998) – but rather one of conflict resolution. Some systems are better equipped to reduce the harmful consequences of conflict than others, and systems with this ability evidence comparatively little violence – perhaps "the occasional slap or push ... but no dangerous assaults or killings." Systems that lack the ability to limit conflict's collateral damage, on the other hand, display enormous amounts of aggression – "not just pushing and slapping, but kicking, beating, biting, gouging, stabbing, and shooting are regular occurrences, everywhere in evidence" (Cooney 1998:20). The street criminal underworld is an obvious example of the latter.

There is evidence that street-based conflict resolution mechanisms once existed in America's inner cities. In important ethnographic work, Anderson (1990) called attention to the mediating role of so-called "old heads," senior members of street culture whose years of experience "on the corner," along with other forms of accumulated social capital, gave them the pull necessary to stymie conflicts before they mushroomed into full-blown confrontations (see also Cooney 1998). These persons did this in a way that allowed disputing factions to save face, so the game was, reputationally speaking, non-zero sum, which is the only way it could work effectively. The virulent crack epidemic that swept through inner cities during the 1980s and early 1990s, coupled with accelerating de-industrialization and social disorganization, eroded the principle sources of the old heads' status, rendering them impotent. Nothing of substance emerged to replace them, and nothing likely will, absent wholesale structural and economic changes that improve the lot of the inner city poor.

Unprecedented economic growth in the 1990s appeared to be poised to do just that. With unemployment at all-time lows, inflation under control, and real wages climbing (United States Department of Labor 1998), legal labor market opportunities opened at a remarkable pace. The absorption of marginalized individuals into that market, however, was only partial. Had the assimilation of those directly responsible for predatory conflict and its violent consequences been more complete, the "crime drop" of the 1990s would likely have been steeper still. But, of course, those individuals were never going to be attractive job candidates. Nor were they likely to be attracted to the low skill, minimum wage jobs realistically available to them. The values that a job requires – subordination, obedience, responsibility, and gratification delay – are antithetical to the street criminal lifestyle: "Misfits in a world that values precise schedules, punctuality, and disciplined subordination to authority, [street criminals] value the autonomy to structure life and work as they wish" (Shover 1991:92). By now, readers undoubtedly have grasped that subordination of any kind is anathema to street criminals, but subordination to the day-to-day constraints of a mundane job represents something especially subjugating. If autonomy is the lifeblood of the streets and the mantle on which offenders hang their reputation, being under someone else's thumb is simply not tenable to them. Meaningful movement away from the criminal lifestyle can never happen unless offenders fundamentally rethink what opportunity is and what it means to them.

Failing that, the best that authorities might hope for is to make street conflicts less lethal by getting firearms out of the hands of would-be criminal disputants. This was a key element of the Boston Gun Project's "Operation Ceasefire," in which the police targeted warring gangs and, using a variety of approaches, communicated the message that gun carrying would not be tolerated. Such a strategy does not require street criminals to grant legitimacy to the police – indeed it could undermine it further and perhaps strengthen the oppositional culture that drives a good deal of street crime – only that they respect the power of the police. Properly targeted at the most dispute-prone offenders and settings, this strategy might help to reduce the consequences of criminal retaliation and, by doing so, perhaps keep it from spiraling out of control (see Kennedy, Braga, and Piehl 2001 and Braga, Kennedy, Piehl, and Waring 2001 for a full description and review of Operation Ceasefire).

## Conclusion

All of us would like to believe in a just world. But inequalities of wealth, status, and prestige guarantee that the benefits of formal justice will be more available to some people than others. For those denied such benefits, achieving justice requires them to take matters into their own hands. Nowhere is this more evident than in the underworld of urban street criminals, where internecine conflict is tolerated by authorities in the belief that combatants are merely getting what they deserve. To be fair, the combatants themselves not only have accepted this state of affairs, they probably welcome it – though no one really knows whether law enforcement's indifference to disputes among street criminals is a response to or a cause of offender hostility. In a sense, though, that is largely beside the point: No formal mechanism for changing offender behavior is available, whereas police behavior is subject to the control of policy and policy makers, at least in theory. If we accept the proposition that much criminal violence is the result of retaliation, then it follows that one way to tackle it is for authorities to take steps to deal with incubating disputes before they escalate, whether or not the disputants seek their help. To do otherwise risks perpetuating a subculture beyond the law, a "violent land" (Courtwright 1996) regulated by the threat and reality of personal vengeance.

# Works Cited

Adler, Patricia A. 1985. *Wheeling and Dealing*. New York: Columbia University Press.

Agar, Michael 1973. *Ripping and Running: A Formal Ethnography of Urban Heroin Addicts*. New York: Seminar Press.

Anderson, Elijah 1999. *Code of the Street*. New York: Norton.

Anderson, Elijah 1990. *Streetwise: Race, class, and change in an urban community*. Chicago: University of Chicago Press.

Arkes, Hal R., and Peter Ayton 1999. "The Sunk Cost and Concorde Effects: Are Humans Less Rational than Lower Animals?" *Psychological Bulletin* 125:591–600.

Bailey, F. Y., and A. P. Green 1999. *Law Never Here: A Social History of African American Responses to Issues of Crime and Justice*. Westport, CT: Praeger.

Baron, Stephen W., David R. Forde, and Leslie W. Kennedy 2001. "Rough justice: Street youth and violence." *Journal of Interpersonal Violence* 16:662–678.

Barreca, Regina 1995. *Sweet revenge: The wicked delights of getting even*. New York: Berkley Publishing Group.

Baskin, Deborah, and Ira Sommers. 1998. *Causalities of Community Disorder: Women's Careers in Violent Crime*. Boulder, CO: Westview Press.

Baumeister, Roy F., and Campbell, W. K. 1999. "The intrinsic appeal of evil: Sadism, sensational thrills, and threatened egotism." *Personality and Social Psychology Review* 3:210–221.

Berkowitz, L. 1993. *Aggression: Its causes, consequences, and control*. New York: McGraw-Hill.

Biernacki, Patrick, and Dan Waldorf 1981. "Snowball Sampling: Problems and Techniques of Chain Referral Sampling." *Sociological Methods and Research* 10:141–63.

Bies, Robert J., and Thomas M. Tripp 2001. "A Passion for Justice: The Rationality and Morality of Revenge." Justice in the Workplace: From Theory to Practice, pp. 197–208, edited by Russell Cropanzano. Mahway, NJ: Lawrence Erlbaum Associates.

Bies, Robert J., and Thomas M. Tripp 1996. "Beyond Distrust: 'Getting Even' and the Need for Revenge." Trust in organizations: Frontiers of theory and research, pp. 246–260, edited by Roderick M. Kramer and Tom R. Tyler. Thousand Oaks, CA: Sage.

Bishop, Donna M. 1984. "Legal and Extralegal Barriers to Delinquency: A Panel Analysis." *Criminology* 22:403–19.

Black, Donald 1993. *The Social Structure of Right and Wrong*. San Diego: Academic Press.

Black, Donald 1983. "Crime as Social Control." *American Sociological Review* 48:34–45.

Black, Donald 1971. "The social organization of arrest." *Stanford Law Review* 35:733–748.

Blau, Peter 1964. *Exchange and power in social life*. New York: Wiley.

Blumstein, Alfred, and Richard Rosenfeld 1998. "Explaining Recent Trends in U.S. Homicide Rates." *Journal of Criminology and Criminal Law* 88: 1175–1216.

Bottcher, Jean 2001. "Social practices of gender: How gender relates to delinquency in the everyday lives of high-risk youths." *Criminology* 39:893–932.

Bottoms, Anthony, and Paul Wiles 1992. "Explanations of Crime and Place." *Crime, Policing and Place: Essays in Environmental Criminology*, pp. 11–35, edited by D. Evans, N. Fyfe, and D. Herbert. London: Routledge.

Bourgois, Philippe. 1996. "In search of masculinity: Violence, respect, and sexuality among Puerto Rican crack dealers in East Harlem." *British Journal of Criminology* 36:412–427.

Bourgois, Philippe. 1995. *In Search of Respect: Selling Crack in El Barrio*. Cambridge, UK: Cambridge University Press.

Braga, Anthony, David Kennedy, Anne Piehl, and Elin Waring 2001. "Measuring the Impact of Project Ceasefire," in *National Institute of Justice, Reducing Gun Violence: The Boston Gun Project's Operation Ceasefire*, Washington, DC: US Government Printing Office.

Bray, Timothy M. 2003. *The effect of socioeconomic disadvantage and racial isolation on neighborhood homicide*. Unpublished doctoral dissertation, University of Missouri – St. Louis.

Broidy, Lisa, and Robert Agnew 1997. "Gender and Crime: A General Strain Theory Perspective." *Journal of Research in Crime and Delinquency* 34:275–306.

Brophy-Baermann, Bryan, and John A. C. Conybeare 1994. "Retaliating against Terrorism: Rational Expectations and the Optimality of Rules versus Discretion." *American Journal of Political Science* 38:196–210.

Brown, Stephen E., Finn-Aage Esbensen, and Gilbert Geis 1996. *Explaining Crime and Its Context (2nd ed.)*. Cincinnati: Anderson.

Canada, Geoffrey 1995. *Fist stick knife gun: A personal history of violence in America*. Boston: Beacon Press.

Clarke, Ronald V., and Derek B. Cornish. 2001. "Rational Choice." In *Explaining Criminals and Crime: Essays in Contemporary Criminological Theory*, pp. 23–42, edited by R. Paternoster and R. Bachman. Los Angeles: Roxbury.

Collison, Mike. 1996. "In search of the high life: Drugs, crime, masculinities, and consumption." *British Journal of Criminology* 36:428–44.

Connell, R. W. 1995. *Masculinities*. Berkeley, CA: University of California Press.

Connell, R. W. 1987. *Gender and Power: Society, the Person and Sexual Politics*. Stanford, CA: Stanford University Press.

Cook, Phillip, and John Laub 1998. "The Unprecendented Epidemic of Youth Violence." In *Crime and Justice: A Review of Research*: Volume 29, pp. 117–153, edited by Michael Tonry and Mark Moore, Chicago: University of Chicago Press.

Cooney, Mark 1998. *Warriors and peacemakers: How third parties shape violence*. New York: New York University Press.

Cota-McKinley, Amy L., William Douglas Woody, and Paul A. Bell 2001. "Vengeance: Effects of gender, age, and religious background." *Aggressive Behavior* 27:343–350.

Courtwright, David 1996. *Violent Land: Single Men and Social Disorder from the Frontier to the Inner City*. Cambridge, MA: Harvard University Press.

Covington, Jeanette 2003. "The violent black male: Conceptions of race in criminological theories." In Hawkins, Darnell, *Violent Crime: Assessing Race and Ethnic Differences*. New York: Cambridge University Press.

Craig, Kellina M. 1999. "Retaliation, Fear, or Rage: An Investigation of African American and White Reactions to Racist Hate Crimes." *Journal of Interpersonal Violence* 14:138–151.

Crick, Nicki R. 2003. "A gender-balanced approach to the study of childhood aggression and reciprocal family influences." In Crouter, Ann C. and Alan Booth (eds). *Children's Influence on Family Dynamics: The Neglected Side of Family Relationships*. Mahwah, NJ: Lawrence Erlbaum Associates.

Crick, Nicki R., Jennifer K. Grotpeter, and Maureen A. Bigbee. 2002. "Relationally and physically aggressive children's intent attributions and feelings of distress for relational and instrumental peer provocations." *Child Development* 73(4):1134–1142.

Cromwell, Paul F., Alan Marks, James N. Olson, and D'Aunn W. Avary 1991. "Group Effects on Decision-making by Burglars." *Psychological Reports* 69:579–588.

Curtis, Richard, and Travis Wendel 2000. "Lockin' Niggas up like it's goin' out of style: The differing consequences of police interventions in Three Brooklyn, New York drug markets." Paper presented at the American Society of Criminology's annual meeting in San Francisco, November 2000.

Daly, Kathleen 1989. "Gender and Varieties of White-Collar Crime." *Criminology* 27:769–79.

Decker, Scott H. and Barrik Van Winkle 1996. *Life in the Gang*. Cambridge, UK: Cambridge University Press.

DeRidder, Richard, Sandra G. L. Schruijer, and John B. Rijsman 1999. "Retaliation to personalistic attack." *Aggressive Behavior* 25:91–96.

Dodge K. A., J. M. Price, J. A. Bachorowski, and J. P. Newman 1990. "Hostile attribution biases in severely aggressive adolescents." *Journal of Abnormal Psychology* 99:385–92.

Durkheim, Emile 1965. *The rules of the sociological method*. S. Solovay and J. Mueller (trans.), edited by G. Catlin. New York: The Free Press.

Dyer, Joel. 2000. *The Perpetual Prisoner Machine: How America Profits from Crime*. Boulder, CO: Westview.

Edgerton, Robert B. 1972. "Violence in East African tribal societies." *Collective Violence*, pp. 159–170, edited by James F. Short, Jr. and Marvin E. Wolfgang. Chicago: Aldine.

Elliott, Delbert S., and Suzanne S. Ageton 1980. "Reconciling race and class differences in self-reported and official estimates of delinquency." *American Sociological Review* 45:95–110.

Erickson, Maynard L., and LaMar T. Empey 1963. "Court records, undetected delinquency, and decision-making." *Journal of Criminal Law, Criminology, and Police Science* 54:454–469.

Exum, M. Lyn 2002. "The application and robustness of the rational choice perspective in the study of intoxicated and angry intentions to aggress." *Criminology* 40:933–966.

Fitness, Julie 2001. "Betrayal, rejection, revenge, and forgiveness: An interpersonal script approach." *Interpersonal Rejection*, pp. 73–103, edited by M. Leary. London: Oxford University Press.

Fleisher, Mark S. 1995. *Beggars and Thieves*. Madison: University of Wisconsin Press.

Freud, Sigmund 1930. *Civilizations and its Discontents*. London: Hogarth.

Fromm, Erich 1973. *The Anatomy of Human Destructiveness*. New York: Holt, Rinehart, and Winston.

Furby, L. 1986. "Psychology and justice." *Justice: Views from the Social Sciences*, pp. 153–204, edited by R. Cohen. New York: Plenum.

Gabriel, Yiannis 1998. "An introduction to the social psychology of insults in organizations." *Human Relations* 51:1329–1354.

Gilligan, Carol. 1982. *In A Different Voice: Psychological Theory and Women's Development*. Cambridge, MA: Harvard University Press.

Glaser, Barney, and Anselm Strauss. 1987. *The Discovery of Grounded Theory*. Chicago: Aldine.

Glassner, Barry 1999. *The Culture of Fear*. New York: Basic Books.

Glassner, Barry, and Cheryl Carpenter 1985. "The Feasibility of an Ethnographic Study of Property Offenders: A Report Prepared for the National Institute of Justice." Washington, DC: National Institute of Justice. Mimeo.

Goldstein, Paul J. 1985. "The Drugs/Violence Nexus: A Tripartite Conceptual Framework." *Journal of Drug Issues* 15:493–506.

Golub, Andrew, and Bruce D. Johnson 1999. "Cohort Changes in Illegal Drug Use among Arrestees in Manhattan: From the Heroin Injection Generation to the Blunts Generation." *Substance Use and Misuse* 34: 1733–1763.

Goode, Erich 1997. *Deviant Behavior (5th ed.)*. Upper Saddle River, NJ: Prentice Hall.

Gould, Roger V. 2003. *Collision of wills: How ambiguity about social rank breeds conflict*. Chicago: University of Chicago Press.

Gouldner, Alvin W. 1960. "The Norm of Reciprocity: A Preliminary Statement." *American Sociological Review* 25:161–178.

Greenberg J. 1993. "Stealing in the name of justice." *Organizational Behavior and Human Decision Processes* 54:81–103.

Hackney, Suzette, David Ashenfelter, and Cecil Angel 2000. "Crime falls in U.S., state." Retrieved from www.freep.com/news/mich/crime8_20000509. html

Hagan, John, and Bill McCarthy 1997. *Mean Streets: Youth Crime and Homelessness*. Cambridge, UK: Cambridge University Press.

Hamm, Mark 2001. *In Bad Company: America's Terrorist Underground*. Boston: Northeastern University Press.

Hanawalt, Barbara A. 1979. *Crime and Conflict in English Communities, 1300–1348*. Cambridge: Harvard University Press.

Hasluck, Margaret 1954. *The Unwritten Law in Albania*. Cambridge, UK: Cambridge University Press.

Heckathorn, Douglas D. 1997. "Respondent-driven sampling: A new approach to the study of social problems." *Social Problems* 44:174–199.

Heimer, Karen, and Stacy DeCoster. 1999. "The gendering of violent delinquency." *Criminology*. 37:277–317.

Herzberger, Sharon D., and Jennifer A. Hall 1993. "Consequences of Retaliatory aggression against Siblings and Peers: Urban Minority Children's Expectations." *Child Development* 64:1773–1785.

Hobbs, Dick. 1994. "Mannish boys: Danny, Chris, crime, masculinity, and business." In Tim Newburn and Elizabeth Stanko (eds). *Just Boys Doing Business? Men, Masculinities, and Crime*. London: Routledge.

Hochstetler, Andy 2001. "Opportunities and decisions: Interactional dynamics in robbery and burglary groups." *Criminology* 39:737–763.

Homans, G. C. 1961. *Social Behavior: Its Elementary Forms*. New York: Harcourt, Brace, and World.

Horowitz, Ruth 1983. *Honor and the American Dream*. New Brunswick, NJ: Rutgers University Press.

Horwitz, Allan V. 1990. *The Logic of Social Control*. New York: Plenum Press.

Humphreys, Laud 1970. *Tearoom Trade*. Chicago: Aldine de Gruyter.

Huston, Ted, Gilbert Geis, and Richard Wright 1976. "The Angry Samaritan." *Psychology Today* 10: 61–64, 85.

Irwin, John 1972. "Particpant Observation of Criminals." In *Research on Deviance*, edited by J. Douglas. New York: Random House.

Jacobs, Bruce A. 1999. *Dealing Crack: The Social World of Streetcorner Selling*. Boston: Northeastern University Press.

Jacobs, Bruce A. 2000. *Robbing Drug Dealers: Violence Beyond the Law*. New York: Aldine de Gruyter.

Jacobs, Bruce A., with Richard Wright 2000. "Researching Drug Robbery." Chapter 1 of *Robbing Drug Dealers: Violence Beyond the Law*. New York: Aldine de Gruyter.

Jacobs, Bruce A., Volkan Topalli, and Richard Wright 2000. "Managing retaliation: Drug robbery and informal sanction threats." *Criminology* 38:171–198.

Jacoby, Susan 1983. *Wild Justice: The Evolution of Revenge*. New York: Harper and Row.

Jenness, Valerie 1993. *Making it Work: The Prostitutes' Rights Movement in Perspective*. New York: Aldine de Gruyter.

Johnson, Eric, and John Payne 1986. "The Decision to Commit a Crime: An information-Processing Analysis." In *The Reasoning Criminal*. Derek B. Cornish and Ronald V. Clarke (eds.) New York: Springer-Verlag, pp. 170–185.

Jones, E. E. and K. E. Davis 1965. "From acts to dispositions: The attribution process in person perception." Advances in experimental psychology, pp. 220–266, edited by L. Berkowitz. New York: Academic Press.

Katz, Jack 1991. "The Motivation of the Persistent Robber." *Crime and Justice: A Review of Research*, pp. 277–305, edited by M. Tonry. Chicago: University of Chicago Press.

Katz, Jack 1988. *Seductions of Crime: Moral and Sensual Attractions in Doing Evil*. New York: Basic Books.

Kennedy, David, Anthony Braga, and Anne Piehl 2001. "Developing and Implementing Operation Ceasefire." In National Institute of Justice, *Reducing Gun Violence: The Boston Gun Project's Operation Ceasefire*, Washington, DC: US Government Printing Office.

Kershnar, Stephen 2001. *Desert, Retribution, and Torture*. Totowa, NJ: Rowman and Littlefield.

Khatri, Naresh, and H. Alvin Ng 2000. "The Role of Intuition in Strategic Decisionmaking." *Human Relations* 53:57–86.

Kim, Sung Hee, Richard H. Smith, and Nancy L. Brigham 1998. "Effects of power imbalance and the presence of third parties on reactions to harm: Upward and downward revenge." *Personality and Social Psychology Bulletin* 24:353–361.

Kim, Sung Hee, and Richard H. Smith 1993. "Revenge and conflict escalation." *Negotiation Journal*. January:37–43.

Lawler, E. J. 1986. "Bilateral Deterrence and Conflict Spiral: A Theoretical Analysis." *Advances in Group Processes*, vol. 3, pp. 107–130, edited by E. J. Lawler. Greenwich, CT: JAI Press.

Lerner, M. J. 1980. *The Belief in a Just World*. New York: Plenum.

Letkemann, Peter 1973. *Crime as Work*. Englewood Cliffs, NJ: Prentice-Hall.

Lewis, I. M. 1961. *A Pastoral Democracy: A Study of Pastoralism and Politics among the Northern Somali of the Horn of Africa*. Oxford: Oxford University Press.

Loftin, Colin 1985 "Assaultive violence as a contagious social process." *Bulletin of the New York Academy of Medicine* 62:550–55.

Loftus, Elizabeth, and Hunter Hoffman 1989. "Misinformation and Memory: The Creation of New Memories." *Journal of Experimental Psychology* 118: 100–104.

Luckenbill, David 1981. "Generating Compliance: The Case of Robbery." *Urban Life* 10:25–46.

Luckenbill, David F. 1977. "Criminal homicide as a situated transaction." *Social Problems* 25:176–186.

Luckenbill, David F., and Daniel P. Doyle 1989. "Structural position and violence: Developing a cultural explanation." *Criminology* 27:419–36.

MacLeod, Jay 1987. *Ain't No Making It.* Boulder, CO: Westview.

Maher, Lisa 1997. *Sexed Work.* New York: Clarendon Press.

Maher, Lisa, and Kathleen Daly 1996. "Women in the street-level drug economy: Continuity or change?" *Criminology* 34:465–492.

Markowitz, F. E., and R. E. Felson 1998. "Social–demographic differences in attitudes and violence." *Criminology* 36:117–138.

Marleau, Jude, and Alayne Hamilton. 1999. "Demanding to Be Heard: Women's Use of Violence." *Humanity and Society* 23:339–358.

Marongiu, Pietro, and Graeme Newman 1987. *Vengeance: The Fight against Injustice.* Totowa, NJ: Rowman and Littlefield.

Meier, Robert F., Leslie W. Kennedy, and Vincent F. Sacco. 2001. "Crime and the criminal event perspective." In *The Process and Structure of Crime,* pp. 1–28, edited by R. F. Meier, L. W. Kennedy, and V. F. Sacco. New Brunswick, NJ: Transaction.

Mercy, James, Mark Rosenberg, Kenneth Powell, Claire Broome, and William Roper 1993. "Public Health Policy for Preventing Violence." *Health Affairs* 12: 7–28.

Merry, Sally Engle 1990. *Getting Justice and Getting Even; Legal Consciousness among Working-Class Americans.* Chicago: University of Chicago Press.

Messerschmidt, James W. 2000. *Nine Lives: Adolescent Masculinities, the Body, and Violence.* Boulder, CO: Westview Press.

Messerschmidt, James W. 1997. *Crime as Structured Action: Gender, Race, Class, and Crime in the Making.* Thousand Oaks, CA: Sage.

Messerschmidt, James W. 1993. *Masculinities and Crime: Critique and Reconceptualization of Theory.* Lanham, MD: Rowman and Littlefield.

Mieczkowski, Thomas 1986. "'Geeking up' and Throwing Down: Heroin Street Life in Detroit." *Criminology* 24:645–666.

Miller, Dale T. 2001. "Disrespect and the experience of injustice." *Annual Review of Psychology* 52:527–553.

Miller, Jerome G. 1996. *Search and Destroy: African-American Males in the Criminal Justice System.* Cambridge, UK: Cambridge University Press.

Miller, Jody. 2002. "The strengths and limits of 'doing gender' for understanding street crime." *Theoretical Criminology.* 6:433–460.

Miller, Jody 2001. *One of the Guys: Girls, Gangs, and Gender*. New York: Oxford University Press.

Miller, Jody 1998. "Up it up: Gender and the accomplishment of street robbery." *Criminology*. 36:37–66.

Miller, Jody, and Norman White. 2003. "Gender and adolescent relationship violence: A contextual examination." *Criminology* 41(4):1207–1248.

Miller, Norman, William C. Pedersen, Mitchell Earlywine, and Vicki E. Pollock. 2003. "A theoretical model of triggered displaced aggression." *Personality and Social Psychology Review* 7:75–97.

Miller, Walter B. 1958. "Lower Class Culture as a Generating Milieu of Gang Delinquency." *Journal of Social Issues* 14:5–19.

Miller, William 1997. "Clint Eastwood and Equity: The Virtues of Revenge and the Shortcomings of Law in Popular Culture." Law and the Domains of Culture, pp. 161–202, edited by Austin Sarat and Thomas Kearns. Ann Arbor: University of Michigan Press.

Miller, William 1993. *Humiliation and Other Essays on Honor, Social Discomfort, and Violence*. Ithaca, NY: Cornell University Press.

Molm, Linda D. 1994. "Is punishment effective? Coercive strategies in social exchange." *Social Psychology Quarterly* 57:75–94.

Moore, Michael S. 1993. "Justifying retributivism." *Israel Law Review* 27:15–49.

Mullins, Christopher 2004. *Masculinities, Streetlife, and Violence*. Unpublished Ph.D. dissertation, University of Missouri-St. Louis.

Mullins, Christopher W., and Richard T. Wright. 2003. "Gender, social networks, and residential burglary." *Criminology* 41:1601–1627.

Nagin, Daniel, and Greg Pogarsky 2001. "Integrating celerity, impulsivity, and extralegal sanction threats into a model of general deterrence: Theory and evidence." *Criminology* 39:865–92.

Nye, F. Ivan, and James F. Short, Jr. 1956. "Scaling delinquent behavior." *American Sociological Review* 22:326–31.

Ohbuchi, Kennichi, and Megumi Saito 1986. "Power imbalance, its legitimacy, and aggression." *Aggressive Behavior* 12:33–40.

Oliver, William 1994. *The Violent Social World of Black Men*. New York: Lexington.

Paternoster, Raymond, and Alex Piquero 1995. "Reconceptualizing Deterrence: An Empirical Test of Personal and Vicarious Experiences." *Journal of Research in Crime and Delinquency* 32:251–286.

Pederson, William C., Candace Gonzales, and Norman Miller 2000. "The moderating effect of trivial triggering provocation on displaced aggression." *Journal of Personality and Social Psychology* 78:913–927.

Peterson, Elicka S.L. 1999. "Murder as self-help: Women and intimate partner homicide." *Homicide Studies* 3:30–46.

Pitt-Rivers, Julian 1966. "Honour and social status." In *Honour and Shame: The Values of Mediterreanean Society*, pp. 19–77, edited by J. G. Peristiany. Chicago: University of Chicago Press.

Polk, Kenneth 1994. *When Men Kill: Scenarios of Masculine Violence.* Cambridge, UK: Cambridge University Press.

Polsky, Ned 1969. *Hustlers, Beats, and Others.* Chicago: Aldine.

Posner Richard A. 1980. "Retribution and related concepts of punishment." *The Journal of Legal Studies* 9:71–92.

Prus, Robert 1984. "Purchasing Products for Resale: Assessing Supliers as 'Partners-in-Trade.'" *Symbolic Interaction* 7:249–278.

Rather, Dan 2001. CBS Evening News. September 12.

Ripstein, Arthur 1997. "Responses to humiliation." *Social Research* **64**: 90–111.

Rosenfeld, Richard, and Scott H. Decker 1996. "Consent to Search and Seize: Evaluating an Innovative Youth Firearm Supression Program." *Law and Contemporary Problems* 59:197–219.

Rosenfeld, Richard, Bruce A. Jacobs, and Richard Wright. 2003. "Snitching and the code of the streets." *British Journal of Criminology* 43:291–309.

Rothschild, Joyce, and Terance D. Miethe, 1999. "Disclosures and Management Retaliation. The Battle to Control Information about Organization Corruption." *Work and Occupations* 26:107–128.

Sampson, Robert J., and Stephen W. Raudenbush 1999. "Systematic Social Observation of Public Spaces: A New Look at Disorder in Urban Neighborhoods." *American Journal of Sociology* 105:603–651.

Sarat, Austin 1997. "Vengeance, victims, and the identities of law." *Social and Legal Studies* 6:163–189.

Schnake, Sherry B. Janet B. Ruscher, Kim Lee Gratz, and Edgar C. O'Neal 1997. "Measure for Measure? Male Retaliation Commensurate with Anger Depends on Provocateur Gender and Aggression Covertness." *Journal of Social Behavior and Personality* 12:937–954.

Seton, Paul H. 2001. "On the importance of getting even: A study of the origins and intention of revenge." *Smith College Studies in Social Work* 72:77–97.

Shaffir, Wiliam B., Robert A. Stebbins, and Allan Turowetz 1980. *Fieldwork Experience: Qualitative Approaches to Social Research,* New York: St. Martin's Press.

Sheley, Joseph F., and James D. Wright. 1995. *In the Line of Fire: Youth, Guns, and Violence in Urban America.* Hawthorne, NY: Aldine de Gruyter.

Sherman, Lawrence 2003. "Reason for emotion: Reinventing justice with theories, innovations, and research – The American Society of Criminology 2002 Presidential Address." *Criminology* 41:1–37.

Sherman, Lawrence 1993. "Defiance, Deterrence, and Irrelevance: A Theory of the Criminal Sanction." *Journal of Research in Crime and Delinquency* 30:445–73.

Shover, Neal 1996. *Great Pretenders.* Boulder, CO: Westview.

Shover, Neal 1991. "Burglary." *Crime and Justice: A Review of Research: Volume 14,* pp. 73–113, edited by Michael Tonry, Chicago: University of Chicago Press.

Sim, Joe 1994. "Tougher than the Rest? Men in Prison." In Tim Newburn and Elizabeth Stanko (eds). *Just Boys Doing Business: Men, Masculinities, and Crime.* New York: Routledge.

Simon, David 1991. *Homicide: A Year on the Killing Streets.* New York: Fawcett Columbine.

Simon, Herbert A. 1979. "Rational decision making in business organizations." *The American Economic Review* 69:493–513.

Simpson, Sally 1991. "Caste, class, and violent crime: Explaining differences in female offending." *Criminology,* 29:115–135.

Simpson, Sally, and Lori Elis. 1995. "Doing gender: Sorting out the caste and crime conundrum." *Criminology.* 33:47–81.

Singer, Simon 1988. "The fear of reprisal and the failure of victims to report a personal crime." *Journal of Quantitative Criminology* 4:289–302.

Solomon, Robert C. 1990. *A Passion for Justice: Emotions and the Origins of the Social Contract.* Reading, MA.: Addison-Wesley.

Solomon, Robert C. 1989. "The emotions of justice." *Social Justice Research* 3:345–374.

Sluka, Jeffrey A. 1990. "Participant Observation in Violent Social Contexts." *Human Organization* 49:109–128.

Spradley, James 1980. *Participant Observation.* New York: Holt, Rinehart, and Winston.

Spreen Marius 1992. "Rare Populations, Hidden Populations, and Link-Tracing Designs: What and Why?" *Bulletin de Méthodologie Sociologique* 6:34–58.

Steffensmeier, Darrell 1983. "Organization properties and sex-segregation in the underworld: Building a sociological theory of sex differences in crime." *Social Forces* 61:1010–1032.

Steffensmeier, Darrell, and Robert Terry. 1986. "Institutional sexism in the underworld: A view from the inside." *Sociological Inquiry* 56:304–323.

Strauss, Anselm 1987. *Qualitative Analysis for Social Scientists.* Cambridge, UK:: Cambridge University Press.

Sutherland, Edwin and Donald Cressey 1970. *Criminology, 8th edition.* Philadelphia: Lippincott.

Sykes, Gresham, and David Matza 1957. "Techniques of Neutralization: A Theory of Delinquency." *American Sociological Review* 22:667–670.

Tedeschi, James T., and Richard B. Felson 1994. *Violence, Aggression, and Coercive Actions.* Washington, DC: American Psychological Association.

Topalli, Volkan, Robert Fornango, and Richard Wright 2002. "Drug dealers, robbery, and retaliation: Vulnerability, deterrence, and the contagion of violence." *British Journal of Criminology* 42:337–351.

Travis, Jeremy, Amy L. Solomon, and Michelle Waul. 2001. *From prison to home: The dimensions and consequences of prisoner reentry.* Washington, DC: Urban Institute.

UCR 2002. *Crime in the United States,* Washington. DC: U.S. Government Printing Office.

United States Department of Labor 1998. Quarterly Report, Washington, DC: US Government Printing Office.

Van Mannen, John 1988. *Tales of the Field: On Writing Ethnography*. Chicago: University of Chicago Press.

Vidmar, Neil 2001. "Retribution and revenge." In *Handbook of Justice Research*, pp. 31–63, edited by Joseph Sanders and V. Lee Hamilton. New York: Kluwer.

Walker, A. and Charles Lidz 1977. "Methodological Notes on the Employment of Indigenous Observers." In *Street Ethnography*, pp. 103–123, edited by R. Weppner. Beverly Hills, CA: Sage.

Wendel, Travis 2000. "Zero Tolerance: Misleading results." *Drug Link* November/December:3–6.

Wenzel, Michael 2001. "A social categorization approach to distributive justice: Social identity as the link between relevance of inputs and need for justice." *British Journal of Social Psychology* 40:315–335.

West, D., and David Farrington 1977. *The Delinquent Way of Life*. London: Heinemann.

West, Candace, and Sarah Fenstermaker. 1995. "Doing difference." *Gender and Society*. 9:3–37.

West, Candace, and Don Zimmerman 1987. "Doing gender." *Gender and Society*. 1:125–151.

West, W.Gordon 1980, "Access to Adolescent Deviants and Deviance," pp. 31–44, in Shaffir, W., R. Stebbins, and A. Turowitz(eds), *Fieldwork Experience: Qualitative Approaches to Social Research*. New York: St. Martin's Press.

White, Jacquelyn, W., and Robin M. Kowalski. 1994. "Deconstructing the myth of the non-aggressive women." *Psychology of Women Quarterly* 18:487–508.

Whyte, William Foote, with Kathleen King Whyte. 1984. *Learning from the Field: A Guide from Experience*. Beverly Hills, CA: Sage.

Wilkinson, Deanna L., and Jeffrey Fagan 2001. "A theory of violent events." pp. 169–195, in R. F. Meier, L. W. Kennedy, and V. F. Sacco (eds.), The Process and Structure of Crime. New Brunswick, NJ: Transaction.

Williams, Christopher R. 2002. "Toward a transvaluation of criminal 'justice;' On vengeance, peacemaking, and punishment." *Humanity and Society* 25:100–16.

Wilson, William J. 1996. *When Work Disappears*. New York: Knopf.

Wolff, K. 1960. Emile Durkheim et al., *Writings on Sociology and Philosophy*. New York: Harper and Row.

Wolfgang, Marvin 1958. *Patterns in Criminal Homicide*. Philadelphia: University of Pennsylvania Press.

Wolfgang, Marvin E., and Franco Ferracuti 1967. *The Subculture of Violence*. London: Tavistock Press.

Wright, Richard T., and Scott H. Decker 1997. *Armed Robbers in Action*. Boston: Northeastern University Press.

Wright, Richard T., and Scott H. Decker 1994. *Burglars on the Job*. Boston: Northeastern University Press.

Wright, Richard, and Michael Stein 1996. "Seeing Ourselves: Exploring the Social Production of Criminological Knowledge in a Qualitative Methods Course." *Journal of Criminal Justice Education* 7:66–77.

Zimring, Franklin E., and Gordon J. Hawkins 1973. *Deterrence: The Legal Threat in Crime Control*. Chicago: University of Chicago Press.

# Index

retaliation, delayed (*see*
  retaliation, calculated)
retaliation direct, 117
retaliation, gendered
  and male-on-male
    and firearms 78
    and women 77
  and male-on-female
    and disregarded slights 82,
      94
    and masculinity 82
    and non-violent tactics 75,
      82, 85–6
  and female-on-female
    and assistance in attacks 91
    and code of streets 86
    and differences from men
      86–7
    and family 87
    and other weapons 91
  and female-on-male
    and male proxies 92, 95
    and non-physical retaliation
      92–3
retaliation, imperfect
  and anger 116
  and retribution 118
  and substituting targets
    101–2
  and third parties 101
  and unjustified retaliation 101
  as alternative 36, 64–5, 119
  definition of 46, 55, 62
  reasons for 62, 64–5, 103
  results of 119
retaliation, marginally imperfect
  and guilt perception 111–12,
    114
  and targets 110, 114
  and victims 102
  as just 118

definition of 102
reasons for 110–11
retaliation, non-
  reasons for 65–7
retaliation, non-violent 87, 88, 95
retaliation, reflexive
  and why not to use 49
  as street justice 1, 46, 47
  definition of 47
retaliation, reflexively displaced
    46, 103–4
retaliation, relationally imperfect
  and family 108, 109–10
  and message sending 108
  and reasons for 108
  and victims 102
  as substitute for direct 108
  as just 118
  definition of 102
retaliation, sneaky
  and deterrence 73
  and excessive violence 60–1
  and symmetry of method 60
  definition of 46, 58
  strategy of 58, 59–60
retaliation, wholly imperfect
  and anger 103
  and drug world 105–6
  and targets 104
  and victims 102
  as just 118
  definition of 102
  reasons for 103, 104, 108
retaliatory proxies
  and anonymity 107
  and counter-retaliation 40
  and family 80–2
  and males for females 92, 95
  as power 80
  disdain for 79–80
  reasons for 43, 61–2

Other books in the series (continued from page iii)